CONTENTS

INTRODUCTION

These are essays that I have written over the past few years that explore several facets of Evolutionary Astrology as taught by Jeffrey Wolf Green. The exploration of these astrological archetypes is informed as well by classic Greek Mythology and astronomy.

The work in general also benefits from the writings of other astrologers including, but not limited to, Liz Green, Howard Sasportas, Brian Clark, Demetra George, Erin Sullivan, Rose Marcus, Patricia Walsh, Dane Rudyhar, and Mark Jones.

Daniel Fiverson
October 2020
Santa Fe, New Mexico

WHAT IS EVOLUTIONARY ASTROLOGY?

E volutionary Astrology describes the journey of the Soul from lifetime to lifetime.

The unique, multidimensional design of planets, stars, and asteroids at the moment of birth contains the symbolic encapsulation of past, present, and *probable* future.

Evolutionary Astrology is a modern, transpersonal, depth psychology, and Soul-centered approach to the ancient craft of astrology. The work builds upon, and adds a spiritual perspective to its foundation in traditional Western Astrology. Evolution is a fact. It is not a theory.

The natal birth chart is a snapshot of the celestial energies that are present at the moment we are born. It contains the entire set of information pertaining to the cycle of lessons that we have brought with us into this lifetime and are wor`king on going forward.

The Principles of Evolutionary Astrology
as Developed by
Jeffrey Wolf Green and Steven Forrest

Evolutionary Astrology embraces paradigms and methodologies which specifically measure the growth of the soul from life to life. These methods invariably focus on the planet Pluto and its relationship to the Nodal Axis. While it is composed of a set of specific formal methodologies, evolutionary astrology is ultimately characterized less by a technical approach than by a set of philosophical principles defined by natural law. Different evolutionary astrologers may use somewhat different interpretive methods, but they can always be recognized by a devotion to the following core perceptions:

1. An acceptance of the fact that human beings incarnate in a succession of lifetimes.

2. An acceptance of the fact that the birthchart reflects the evolutionary condition of the soul at the moment of incarnation.

3. An acceptance of the fact that the birthchart reflects the evolutionary intentions of the soul for the present life.

4. An acceptance of the fact that the circumstances of the present life, both materially and psychologically, do not arise randomly, but rather reflect the evolutionary intentions and necessities of the soul.

5. An acceptance of the fact that human beings interact creatively and unpredictably with their birthcharts; that all astrological symbols are multi-dimensional and are modulated into material and psychic expression by the consciousness of the individual.

6. An acceptance of the fact that human beings are responsible for the realities they experience, both internally and externally.

7. A respectful intention to accept and support a person seeking astrological help, regardless of the evolutionary state in which such an individual finds himself or herself.

Courtesy Jeffrey Wolf Green School of Evolutionary Astology

The natal birth chart is a snapshot of the celestial energies that are present at the moment we are born. It contains the entire set of information pertaining to the cycle of lessons that we have brought with us into this lifetime, and are continuing to work on going forward. Our birth chart holds the memories and impressions of past accomplishment as the gifts that we have brought with us into this lifetime.

Pluto In The Birth Chart: The Soul's Dual Desire Nature

 Pluto in a birth chart correlates to the Soul -- the Wave that instinctively separates from the Ocean of Source, All-That-Is, God/Goddess, or however you perceive that which we are part of that is greater than ourselves; the Higher Power that is the Creative force of the Universe.

The Soul's core desire is for security. Pluto correlates to where we will find our deepest source of the knowledge of self, and the safety that understanding provides.

Pluto, correlates to our karma as well as our DNA -- the necessities we have brought with us that empower the self-actualization process. Karma is simply choice. The choices that we make in each moment of time. We reap what we sow; the principle of cause and effect. It is neither punishment, nor retribution, just simply the "unfinished business" which has carried over into this lifetime to be completed and resolved.

In that regard, the Soul has a dual desire nature. The first desire of the Soul is to separate from Source and to experience the Self from every possible perspective and experience, through direct emotional experience. The Soul enters into Time and Space in order to experience and learn about itself through all of its human experiences. We have heard the well known meme:

> "We are not humans having a spiritual experience. We are spiritual beings having a human experience."

Creation of Adam by Michelangelo Buonarroti

The Soul is a wave in the Ocean of All-That-Is. As we individuate from Source the illusion of separation is created. The wave no longer sees itself as part of the Ocean, but only as the wave.

> "The wave is the same as the ocean, though it is not the whole ocean. So each wave of creation is a part of the eternal Ocean of Spirit. The Ocean can exist without the waves, but the waves cannot exist without the Ocean."
>
> ~~ Paramahansa Yogananda

Security is realized through the saturation with Earthly experience — learning through the 5 senses about gender, culture, ethnicity, religion, poverty, wealth, health, illness, and so on.

> "We are not human beings having a spiritual experience. We are spiritual beings having a human experience."
> –Teilhard de Chardin

The Great Wave of Kanagawa by Katsushika Hokusai

Progressively, the Soul exhausts one separating desire after another, relationships and sexuality, material possessions of every imaginable kind, beauty and artistic creativity, family, power, career... the list goes on and on. As each desire is fulfilled a temporary sense of satisfaction is achieved, but then an even bigger satisfaction is needed. Ultimately the realization arises... *"There must be something more than this."*

The Soul sees that none of the prizes and rewards of the material world, no achievement or acquisition is as fulfilling or as satisfying as was expected.
As this awareness increases, the second, very singular desire of the Soul begins to emerge-- the desire to reconnect to Source; remembering that the wave is simply a part of the ocean, and that the ocean is contained within the wave.

This the realization that the only true fulfillment of the Soul is the awareness of one's connection to Source, and to seek security only through that connection. The process is very gradual. It does not happen in one day, or one year, or even in one lifetime. The dual desires are constantly in a delicate balance. Eventually the balance tips with the human experience of Time and Space.

Someone one once asked Ram Dass,

"How long does it take to attain spiritual enlightenment?"

He answered, (paraphrased)

> "Imagine a mountain, 4 miles high, 4 miles wide, 4 miles deep. Once a year an eagle flies over the top holding a piece of silk in his talon that brushes the top of the mountain. How long will it take for the mountain to be worn down?" --Ram Dass

We have 2 egos, Soul Ego and subjective ego. The evolutionary path forward is toward the balance and unity of the two.

The Relationship Of Mars And Pluto

Mars and Pluto share rulership of the sign of Scorpio. Mars was the ruler until the discovery of Pluto in 1930.

Pluto carries the Soul's deepest unconscious security desires. Mars represents how the individual consciously acts to fulfill those deepest desires. Mars is considered to be the lower octave of Pluto.

Pluto says, "Jump!" Mars says, "How high?"

For this reason, Mars is considered to be the leading edge of our evolution. Mars correlates to what we consciously pursue instinctively, relative to Pluto's core needs for security. If the Soul intends to achieve spiritual enlightenment, Mars will choose the path that leads to the spiritual teacher and pathway. If the Soul desires more saturation in materiality, Mars will seek fame and fortune. There is no judgement. Consciousness has the properties of water. It must fill up every space it passes through before it can move on.

We engage emotionally with each of our desires as we experience them. This is the Soul learning about itself, what it needs, and where it finds meaning in life. Over many cycles of lifetimes we work through sets of lessons. From lifetime to lifetime, we pick up where we left off.

Evolutionary States

According to Jeffrey Wolf Green, there are 3 main evolutionary states -- consensus state, individuated state, and spiritualized state. Each of the states is composed of 3 substages. An individual may be working solely through one evolutionary state, or transitioning from one state to the next.

Allan Swart "Moody Curvy Piano Keys"

Since we are conscious, we are not "pinned" to a single point in this evolutionary spectrum. It is more like playing a chord on a piano, several notes at a time across the wide expanse of possible notes to play -- an arc of the potentials of human experience.

Perhaps we are holding onto something that we still enjoy on a physical level, or still need to find acceptance and approval among our peers (consensus), while we are individuating, or even spiritualizing.

It is important to note that an individual's evolutionary state cannot be determined simply by reading the chart alone. The chart can only be understood from the actual context of an individual's life story. The planetary archetypes have a wide spectrum of expression. For instance, the impact of the planet Neptune for the sign of Pisces in a chart could be indicative of poetic visions or chronic alcoholism. The chart itself does not reveal which way it is working. Only observation and correlation, dialogue and anecdotal conversation can begin to solve the astrological puzzle of the natal birth chart.

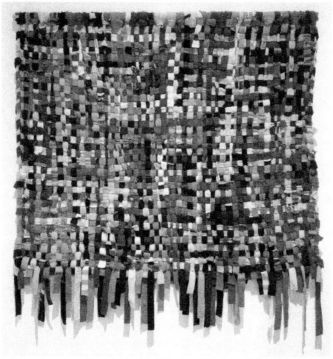

Contextual Data," Aneesa Shami, 2017, woven felt strips.
Courtesy photo / Jeff Davis & Aneesa Shami

Understanding the evolutionary state of the person seeking the reading, by observation and correlation, is essential to understanding how the astrological archetypes are being expressed in any particular lifetime. The dynamics of each archetypal theme are determined by the evolutionary state of the Soul. For instance, we know that Pisces can be either the visionary or the lunatic, and anything in between. This cannot be determined from the chart alone. The chart must be correlated to the life experiences of the individual.

Consensus State

Consensus state comprises approximately 70% of the people on the planet. Jeffrey Green called this the "herd mentality" state. An individual in a consensus state finds security in being like everyone else. They want to "get ahead"... learn "how to play the game" and "to keep up with the Joneses."

In the 3rd stage consensus (at the top of this consensus state) are the people running the world, the bankers, the kings, religious leaders, the lawmakers and political leaders, captains of industry, etc. Over many lifetimes they "have figured it all out". Not only have they learned "how to play the game," they are making the rules. Even as we achieve a maximum of financial and/or social status, we can still not feel secure. We fear that somehow we will lose it all. The more material we accumulate, the more we can lose. The more status we gain, the farther we can fall. We begin to ask ourselves...

There must be something more.

Individuals who are in a consensus state, evolving into the individuated state will perhaps still look and dress the same as everyone else, keep their day job, and continue to lead a "normal" life. But at night they might attend an astrology talk, or have a tarot reading, or perhaps explore meditation and metaphysical teachings.

Rahel Kapsaski "Ramsey Dukes"

Consensus evolutionary state correlates to Saturn, Capricorn, and the 10th House. Security is being like everyone else. Fitting into the framework of society easily and learning to navigate its heights. According to Jeffrey Wolf Green, approximately 70% of the Earth's population are in a consensus state.

Individuated State

After many lifetimes of accepting the cultural and societal conditioning, the Soul begins to realize that the true nature of reality is perhaps different than what our parents, teachers, religious leaders, kings and political leaders have told us.

Carl Jung called this the process of Individuation.

> "I will try to explain the term "individuation" as simply as possible. By it I mean the psychological process that makes a human being an "individual, unique, indivisible unit or "whole man."
>
> --C. G. Jung "The Meaning of Individuation"

They stop believing "the party line" and begin to question authority in order to come to their own conclusions
about the nature of the world. They are the rebels, the innovators"... the free and independent thinkers.

In the individuated third stage of this evolutionary state are the poets, the artists, and the visionaries -- the creative force inspiring humanity to reach higher. This group comprises approximately 20 percent of the planet.

Pablo Picasso, Femme au béret orange et au col de fourrure

The Individuated State correlates to Uranus, Aquarius, and the 11 House. The crystallization of thought and belief that occurred in a consensus state is interrupted, disrupted, even shattered, by the questioning of the true nature of reality, of what is true or real through direct emotional experience.

As a result of the questioning the freedom to think as an individual begins to emerge, the we begin to understand that there are natural laws that are absolute and true outside of time and space -- laws of nature that are true in any time frame of history or culture.

Spiritualized State

As we begin to understand and live according to natural law, we begin the ultimate reconnection to Source.

Spiritual in this context does not mean religious. Most of the world's great religions belong to the consensus state -- evidenced by the patriarchal conditioning that has persisted for the last 6000 years. Souls who are spiritualizing comprise a mere 3-5% of the population of the planet.

The Spiritualized State correlates to Neptune, Pisces, and the 12th House. This is the Reconnection. According to David Hawkins, author of Power v. Force, the power of human consciousness is so great, that in the total history of the planet only a handful of individuals -- Buddha, Jesus, Moses, Yogananda, Gandhi, to name a few, the truly self-realized Masters, have upheld all of mankind. This is the power of consciousness that increases geometrically, not arithmetically. These are the 3rd stage spiritual souls.

The Soul's Evolutionary Intention

Our birth chart reveals our evolutionary axis -- our individual life path forward. All of the astrological archetypes are polarities according to the Hermetic principle of The Law of Polarities--knowledge left to us by the Ancients. The polarity point of Pluto, it's opposite point in the birth chart, correlates to the resolution point of the life's lessons, and our evolutionary intentions.

The South Node of the Moon and its ruler reveal the emotional nature of how those personal lunar (ego) dynamics and processes have functioned to the past. The Lunar North Node and its ruler point the way forward toward our *probable* future. A future that is seeded, but only fulfilled by *choices* (Mars) made in the present.

The circumstances and the relationships we will meet in each lifetime have been chosen by the Soul/Higher Self prior to birth. Free will is expressed by how we respond or react to those circumstances and relationships as they show up.

It's all good. It is not what happens to us. It is about how we respond to what happens that makes it "good" or "bad.

Everything is in a constant state of change, evolution. Perhaps we need to acknowledge that Creation itself is still evolving. If not, then how could a perfect creator create anything that is so perfectly imperfect as our world?

The answer is the the Creator is evolving with and through us.

We are truly stardust.

FROM ETERNAL CHILD TO SAGE:THE MYTHOLOGY, ASTRONOMY, AND EVOLUTIONARY ASTROLOGY OF MERCURY

Jake Baddeley "Hermes"

The astrology of Mercury traces the evolutionary growth of Hermes as puer aeternus to senex. In Jungian terms from eternal child to sage. In Jungian psychology the term *puer aeternus* is used to describe a certain type of man -- charming, affectionate, creative and ever in pursuit of his dreams.

These are the men who remain adolescent well into their adult years. Through the development of the archetype of Hermes/Mercury, *puer* becomes a *senex*, wise sage, an archetype as described by Carl Jung, as well as a classic literary figure. The wise old man can be a profound philosopher distinguished for wisdom and sound judgment. The sage. In the evolution of Mercury, the eternal child becomes the magician.

When astrologers talk about Mercury, the conversation tends to frame the conversation in terms of "how we think" and "how we communicate". We reference cognitive skills and intellect, the quality and tone of the voice, and so on.

The planet Mercury is often reduced in status or importance in the planetary hierarchy because of his rapid speed and diminutive size.

There is however much that is hidden in this deeply personal archetype. He embodies a rich multivalent nature. In fact, this prevalent reductionist approach is a good example of Mercury's cleverness, already working to convince us that what we see is perhaps all there is.

Mercury guides us across the threshold between light and shadow, the conscious and the unconscious, performing the alchemical synthesis of self that we call personal evolution.

When we explore Mercury from mythological, astrological, and astronomical perspectives, meaning emerges that reveals the diversity of ways that Mercury expresses through the natal chart.

The mythology, astronomy, and astrology of this quixotic character reveals a much deeper story. As Mercury shuttles back and forth in close proximity to the Sun, he disseminates the "messages" received from the Sun, source of the self-actualizing life force in our solar system.

There is no single mythological thread that connects the various faces and personalities of Mercury, or Hermes as he was known to the Greeks. In one form or another, the mythology of Mercury extends back to earliest oral and written traditions, and spans multiple cultures.

The mythos surrounding Hermes spans eight centuries. We know him primarily from the mythos of Greece and Rome, who were influenced by the earlier Sumerian, Babylonian, and Egyptian cultures. To the Egyptians he was Thoth, to the Romans he was Mercury, the Celts he was Lugh, and to the Norse he was Loki.

The Mythology Of Mercury

The celestial role that he performs is neither accidental nor coincidental. According to Greco-Roman mythology, Hermes/ Mercury was the messenger, brother, traveler, guide, trader, orator, magician and mystic. He was also known to be the trickster, thief, liar, and even rapist. He was not just a messenger; he was the Messenger of the Gods.

He was also the psychopomp, the guide of souls between the worlds of the living and the dead. On the mundane level he was also somebody's sibling, part of a family constellation, just like many of us.

Mercury performs a critical evolutionary role for each of us as he guides us across the boundary between our own light and shadow, the conscious and the unconscious, so that we can perform the alchemical synthesis of self that we call personal evolution.

The earliest accounts present Hermes of Arcadia, a shepherd who tended his flock and lived a bucolic life peacefully on the side of Mount Kyllene. According to this account he was the god of animal husbandry, cattle herding, shepherding, goat herding and even the breeding of horses and mules. In this role he is portrayed as more feminine than masculine, nurturing, living close to the land.

As the mythos evolves a different storyline emerges. His exploits in The Iliad and The Odyssey reveal a more masculine, patriarchal persona.

Homer dubbed him the "giant killer". There are two stories as well where Hermes becomes the rapist of two different princesses. He had no remorse for the death of one of them as a result of what he had done, reflecting his irresponsible *puer aeternus* personality.

The Greek poets Hesiod and Homer tell us:

> "[Hermes] whom Maia bare, the rich-tressed Nymphe, when she

was joined in love with Zeus,--a shy goddess, for she avoided the company of the blessed gods, and lived within a deep, shady cave.

There Kronion [Zeus] used to lie with the rich-tressed Nymphe, unseen by deathless gods and mortal men, at dead of night while sweet sleep should hold white-armed Hera fast.

And when the purpose of great Zeus was fixed in heaven, she was delivered and a notable thing came to pass. For then she bare a son, of many shifts, blandly cunning, a robber, a cattle driver, a bringer of dreams, a watcher by night, a thief at the gates, one who was soon to show forth wonderful deeds among the deathless gods. Born with the dawning, at mid-day he played on the lyre, and in the evening , ihe stole the cattle of far-shooting Apollon on the fourth day of the month; for on that day queenly Maia bare him."

Hermes And The Stolen Cattle

The best known is the tale of Hermes's theft of the cattle that belonged to his half-brother Apollo.

The story goes that only one day after his birth, Hermes was bored with his crib, so he turned himself into a puff of vapor and slipped through a keyhole in the door to find adventure.

Percy Jackson "Hermes stealing Apollo's Cattle"

He soon came upon his brother's cattle and instantly decided that he needed to have some of them for his own. So he spirited them away by making it look like they had walked backwards, obscuring the direction they had gone, and fashioning magical sandals for himself that would erase his tracks.

On his way, he came upon a tortoise whose lustrous shell intrigued him. Hermes cleverly persuaded the tortoise to let him pick him up to have a closer look, upon which Hermes immediately and shamelessly cracked open the shell, and ate the tortoise meat. Then, using sinews from the cows he had stolen from his brother, Hermes fashioned the shell into a lyre. His first adventure completed, Hermes then returned home to his cradle.

His brother, oracular Sun God Apollo soon divined what had happened and confronted his newborn brother with the theft. Hermes argued "I am just a baby. How could I have possibly conceived such a complex and devious act?"

Not satisfied with his younger brother's fable, Apollo brought the case to their father Zeus for resolution. Hermes again pleaded his case of being incapable of such a duplicitous act.

Zeus was so taken with the hubris and cleverness of his young son, that he recused himself from judgement and commanded the two siblings to work it out between themselves.

Apollo had heard Hermes playing his newly created lyre and was captivated by its melodious sound. Sensing that he must obey his father and as recompense Apollo for attempting to steal his cattle, Hermes offered his lyre to Apollo as a gift. Apollo accepted the gift graciously, Hermes returned the stolen cattle, and the two brothers reconcile their differences. Happy ending.

> "As for honors I'm going to get in on the same ones that is sacred to Apollo. If my father won't stand for I'll still try. I'm capable certainly to be thief number one."
>
> --Homeric Hymn to Hermes

Puer Aeternus

This concept was popularized by psychologist Dan Kiley, in his 1983 book, <u>The Peter Pan Syndrome: Men Who Have Never Grown Up</u>. Like the famous character in the J. M. Barrie play, many of the troubled teenage boys he treated and had problems growing up and acceping adult responsibilities. This trouble continued on into adulthood.

As the expression of the *puer aeternus,* in the natal chart, Mercury reveals where we feel young at heart, and describes our sense of humor and how we like to play.

There is an inherent natural curiosity. Along with the refusal to

Je crois qu'il profita, pour son évasion, d'une migration d'oiseaux sauvages.

grow up, an individual expressing as puer aeterna will be often be prone to superficiality of response and expression. Thinking and opinion is often reductionist. There is dishonesty and an obfuscation of the truth in order to retain one's own established self-identification. There is no evidence of conscience displayed, as there is little regard for the consequences of action or speech. The child-man who refuses to grow up and meet the responsibilities and challenges of life face on, waiting instead for his ship to come in and solve all his problems. The individual displays glibness. They gloss over matters of import and lie to hide the truth. There is often a total disregard of the consequences of their actions.

> "Quite often, people with an underdeveloped Mercury can be concerned with dissemination of superficial factual knowledge and with compartmentalizing ideas, holding unopposable opinions and refusing to be influenced by human values and emotions because these are too subjective to be tested against external reality."
>
> --Freda Edis "The God Between: A Study of Astrological Mercury "

Mercury's Gifts

In the exchange of his lyre, Apollo favors Hermes with the gift of divination, leading him to discover astronomy, astrology and mathematics. Hermes uses these abilities to order and enumerate the phenomena of the natural world with the alphabet and numbers. Hermes also receives through divination the art of magic, which grants him invisibility and other powers.

The myth of the stolen cattle highlights the archetypal sibling relationship between Hermes and Apollo. Both brothers are jealous. The older brother Apollo being jealous of the attention given to the newest member of the family, and the younger brother Hermes being jealous of the status, power, privilege, and possessions of his elder brother.

> "The Hermes/Mercury archetype and the third house is to experience lying, cheating, gossiping and teasing among the siblings in our experience to be recognized and separate.
>
> --Brian Clark "The Family Legacy

Challenging aspects from Chiron, Saturn, or Pluto to Mercury can often indicate sibling rivalries and family disconnects.

The Caduceus

Zeus was so impressed and proud of the verbal craftiness and ingenuity of his newborn son, that he appoints him to be the messenger of the gods, and bestows upon him a magical golden staff to facilitate his work.

Some accounts suggest that the oldest known imagery of the caduceus have their roots in Mesopotamian origin with a Sumerian god whose symbol, a staff with two snakes intertwined around it, dates back to 4000 to 3000 BCE.

By some accounts the caduceus evolved from a rod entwined with a single snake that was carried by Asclepius, known as the father of modern medicine.

Hermes used the caduceus to help Heracles capture Cerberus, the monstrous watchdog with three (or by some accounts fifty) heads, which guarded the entrance to Hades, by putting him to sleep.

He used his wand to aid Priam, to lull the guards to sleep so that he could retrieve the slain and defiled body of Hector from Achilles' camp in <u>The Iliad.</u>

Hermes put the giant Argos to sleep in the guise of Argeiphontes, so that he could slay him, becoming the "giant killer". Argos was called Argos Panoptes, meaning "Ëœeall seeing'. He had eyes all over his body to better guard his flocks.   The killing of the herdsman Argos was not an easy task and Hermes became famous for killing him.

He saved Odysseus from Circe by giving him the magical herb "moly" that made him immune to her enchantments.

Caduceus was the staff carried by Hermes Trismegistus in Greco-Egyptian mythology. This theme of magic re-emerges in the myths of the Hellenistic period as Hermes is syncretized with the Egyptian god Thoth.

Hermes, the Greek god of interpretive communication, was combined with Thoth, the Egyptian god of wisdom, to become Hermes Trismegistus, Hermes Thrice Great, patron of astrology and alchemy. Both Hermes and Thoth were gods of writing. In addition, both gods were psychopomps, guiding souls to the afterlife.

Psychopomp ~ Guide Of Souls

The Souls of Acheron, by Adolf Hiremy-Hirschl 1898

As the messenger of the gods, Hermes was the only god who could enter and leave the underworld without harm. He was a psychopomp -- a guide of souls between worlds.

The best-known account is the story of his rescue of Persephone, after her abduction by Hades.

Hermes also aided Orpheus, the legendary musician, poet, and prophet in ancient Greek religion and myth, in the retrieval of his wife Eurydice who had descended into the underworld.

Hermes also guided the slain warriors of the Trojan War down into Hades.

The Influence Of Hellenism

By the late 1st Century BCE, the center of Greek learning and knowledge had migrated to Alexandria, the city Alexander the Great built in his own name at the fertile delta of the Nile River.

Under the tutelage of Claudius Ptolemy, writer, mathematician, astronomer, geographer, poet, and astrologer, alchemy, astrology, Kabbalah, and tarot the foundations of the metaphysics, began to emerged would flow through the occult world for the next 2000 years.

Alchemy refers to:
~The process of "the transmutation of "base metals" (e.g., lead) into 'noble' ones (particularly gold)
~The creation of an elixir of immortality
~The creation of a panacea able to cure any disease;
~The development of an alkahest--a universal solvent.

The perfection of the human body and soul was thought to permit or result from the alchemical magnum opus and, in the Hellenistic and western tradition, the achievement of gnosis--the Greek word for knowledge and the insight into man's real nature as Divine.

Hermes Trismegistus

It was during this period that the Magician/Alchemist appears as Hermes Trice Anointed. It is not known if he was an actual or mythic figure. I prefer to err on the side of the mythic, which holds so much more latitude and density than the perception of an actual personage could.

Hermes Trismegistus is the syncretization of Hermes and the Egyptian Wisdom God Thoth. A suggestion of the meaning of "thrice anointed" is derived from statements in the Emerald Tablet of Hermes Trismegistus, that he knows the three parts of the wisdom of the whole universe--the three parts being alchemy, astrology, and theurgy.

The puer aeternus, Latin for eternal child, revealed in the mythos of Hermes as liar and thief, has now evolved into the senex, Latin for old person, the wise old man or sage. Puer aeternus and senex are both archetypes described by Carl Jung.

The Astrology Of Mercury

All of the preceding astronomy and mythology informs the astrology of Mercury.

What is it then that is the astrological/alchemical function that Hermes/Mercury correlates to in the natal chart? The nature of Mercury/Gemini/Virgo is connected in the natural zodiac to the mutable cross:

3rd House/Gemini | 6th House/Virgo,
9th House/Sagittarius |12th House/Pisces

There is a natural conflict between left-brain, (Mercury/Gemini) rational inductive reasoning, essentially our opinions and subjective ideas regarding reality, and right brain deductive reasoning, our broader understanding and beliefs regarding the nature of reality (Jupiter/Sagittarius). There is also a conflict between our individual, practical considerations (Mercury/Virgo) and larger transpersonal universal truths (Neptune/Pisces).

image © Daniel Fiverson

We know that Hermes travels between the 3 worlds: the upper

world of divinity, the middle world, our consensus time and space reality, and the lower world, the subconscious.

> "The ability of mediating and moving freely between different contradictory realms (for example the heavens and the under-world) was one of the chief attributes of the Greek Hermes. In alchemy, it was in the hermetic vessel where the spiritual regen-eration and rebirth took place as the intellect was blended with passions and emotions."
>
> --https://symbolreader.net/2014/08/08/in-the-heart-of-the-supreme-mind-thoth-hermes-trismegistus

Hermes can navigate through these three realms without harm. In the same way, we can learn how to navigate through our own personal underworld by understanding the placement of Mer-cury in the natal chart. We can explore and synthesize our own shadow, holistically healing a fractured and dismembered

> "Whatever is not conscious will be experienced as fate."
>
> --C.G. Jung

Mercury's planetary nodes also reveal an archetypal pathway from the Soul's past Mercurial experiences to the future poten-tials held, anchored in the present by Mercury's natal place-ment.

Light cast upon the subconscious reveals, acknowledges and fa-cilitates the release of whatever lies below. The evolutionary journey of the soul embraces the ongoing process of synthesiz-ing conscious and unconscious into a holistic self.

This alchemy of light and shadow removes the impediments to the flow of life force. When conscious and subconscious are fully integrated with solar life force, these self-actualizing ener-gies can be received and absorbed more readily and flow (Moon) more easily throughout the 4 bodies (spiritual, emotional, mental, and physical) without internal psychic or emotional obstruction or distortion.

"The role of Mercury is that it correlates in the human consciousness to the need to give order and linear structure to
the nature of the phenomenal reality. What we call the senses
are an extension of consciousness into the physical body. It is
through the senses that thought and perceptions are ignited in
consciousness. That which is ignited through the senses induces
thoughts."
–Jeffrey Wolf Green

Mercury Retrograde

There is more retrospection and reflection in thought -- looking backwards and going inwards during the retrograde cycle of
Mercury. This phase is perhaps the best known celestial event.
It is said to cause disruptions to all forms of communication
and travel. More importantly it holds the potential for the
introspection and self-reflection that is key to personal growth.

The liminality of the Mercurial archetype is enhanced as we can
feel "betwixt and between". It has been said that if Mercury rises
before the Sun you think first and then act. If the Sun rises before
Mercury you speak first and then seek a justification for your
actions.

The Sun Mercury Cycle

Because of their close proximity, the only aspect or phase relationship that is possible between the Sun and Mercury is the
conjunction, and the new and balsamic phases.

Mercury is never more than 28° from the Sun. Mercury's close
proximity to the Sun correlates directly to his role as the Messenger of the Gods. As he shuttles back and forth he collects and
disseminates astrological solar energy.

There are two types of Sun-Mercury conjunctions, the inferior conjunction when Mercury is retrograde and closest to the Earth, and the superior conjunction when Mercury is direct, opposing the Earth on the far side of the Sun.

The Sun-Mercury cycle begins at the inferior conjunction. During the retrograde Mercury phase the seed thoughts for the cycle are gestated and released.

> "Those natives born with Sun conjunct Mercury are expressive as speakers and writers. There is a strong need to have a voice in the world in one form or another. The new phase relationship with the Sun correlates to Mercury as the morning star, moving ahead of the Sun. This is an individual with an active, initiative mind, always on the lookout for something new to consider, explore, and learn about."
> --Michael R. Meyer A Handbook for Humanistic Astrology

At the superior conjunction, these seed thoughts take shape as ideas and mental associations that shape the unfolding of the waning cycle of this planetary cycle.

In the waxing portion of the cycle, Meyer described this placement as Mercury Prometheus -- after the god who stole fire from Zeus and who took on the role as agent for the benefit, welfare, and advancement of mankind. This Mercury is forward looking, anticipating the future, thinking ahead.

Meyer continues,

> "Born anew from the cycle just closing, the Mercurial faculties of mind and communication have been impressed with a new quality of will, purpose and energy -- symbolized by the zodiacal and house positions of the inferior conjunction which inaugurated the new cycle."

Mercury "steps down" the intense situations generated energies by the outer planets to levels at which they can be understood, recognized, and creatively engaged.

As Mercury meets up with the Sun at their superior conjunction, the Epimethean profile of Mercury emerges, correlating to

Mercury's affinity and rulership in Virgo--Yin, inward directed, and Earth-bound.

> "The role of Mercury is that it correlates in the human consciousness to the need to give order and linear structure to the nature of the phenomenal reality. What we call the senses are an extension of consciousness into the physical body. It is through the senses that thought and perceptions are ignited in consciousness. That which is ignited through the senses induces thoughts."--Jeffrey Wolf Green

Mercury And The Moon

The Moon and superior planets, (Mars through Pluto and the dwarf planets beyond) which reside beyond the Earth's orbit, connect with Mercury across the full spectrum of aspects and phases.

Mercury aspects to the Moon refer to how emotions are integrated with thoughts and vocal expression.

Trines, sextiles, and quintiles will facilitate the ability to express how one is feeling emotionally.

Conjunctions, squares, oppositions, sesquiquadrates, and quincunxes will refer to places where this natural expression is being blocked or distorted in some way. This can be a conflict between head and heart. Often this is an indication of a deeper karmic complex that is being exposed for healing.

Mercury And Venus

Mercury and Venus also travel in a narrowly defined space, never more than 76° apart, only allowing for the conjunction, semisextile, semisquare, and sextile.

A Mercury/Venus blend can bring a beautiful singing or speaking voice, or a beautiful manner of expression via the written word, either as prose or poetry. It is often an individual who is affable, and generally relates well to and gets along with others because they are not prone to disagreements or conflicting opinions. In consort with Venus, our thoughts, ideas, and opinions are innately connected to our values and priorities. One necessarily follows the other. In essence we are what we think and the priorities that we set for ourselves are a direct result of the cognitive structure of the world around us.

The facilitating aspects will "make our intentions clear". Our values and priorities will define the context of how and what we are communicating. There will be a tendency to speak to what has real meaning for us individually and our words will state our priorities very clearly.

The challenging aspects can potentially spin our words and thoughts in a negative direction, feeling jealous, or holding onto vain self-identification. We may even lash out verbally rather than be able to objectively disagree with someone else.

Mercury And Mars

Mercury Mars natives are prone to impulsive and sometimes hurtful speech. Harsh words can create conflict and this planetary combo is ready for any verbal rumble. In general there is self-centeredness about the native and they are often "in their head". Even with challenging aspects though, Mars and Mercury will enliven any conversation, with a spark of wit and intelligence.

The mind is quick and very curious.
"Words have wings"

--Rosicrucian proverb

Mercury And Jupiter

Mercury Jupiter natives frequently possess largesse of jovial good nature and playfulness. They are generally broad-minded, within their own intellectual boundaries; they can be a "bottomless pit" of knowledge, always seeking out new thoughts and ideas. They can be as funny and as fun to be with as they are wordy and long winded. They often have extensive vocabularies.

In their shadow lurks the demons of evangelism, and they often play the role of crusader.

Mercury And Saturn

Mercury and Saturn correlate to the elder teacher whose authoritative voice maintains the status quo. Speech and voice can have a minimalist quality, yet it is filled with authority and importance. The mind is focused and goal oriented. These individuals take their time and think things through.

In its shadow a Mercury Saturn native will often display self-expression that is repressed or suppressed. There can be a tendency to limit one's imagination and fantasy, anything seeming to be too irrational in any way.

There may be insecurity about how smart or skillful someone might feel, but they are still willing to work hard to learn or make it happen.

Their thinking is most conventional though and there is resistance to anything unconventional, not "tried and true."

Mercury And Uranus

Mercury is the lower mind. Uranus is the higher mind. Together they amplify the channel between the two octaves. Individuals can be prone to idealistic thinking as well as practical inspiration. Sleep patterns can be disturbed because of the almost incessant internal chatter. Its best expression is an insightful illuminated mind, futurist, forward thinking, and original.

Depending on the aspects to the rest of the chart, and especially the placements of the Saturn, Neptune, and Pluto, there can be information overload, thoughts and ideas that come faster than they can be assimilated, sentences aren't finished, the native often finding themselves in a general state of TMI. To others the mental gymnastics might seem too "far out", impractical, and unworkable.

Mercury And Neptune

Mercury Neptune natives can be blessed with the most imaginative minds filled with romantic, even surreal imagery. They can be highly intuitive and perceptive, even psychic. They can be extremely compassionate and empathetic. These are the poets, storytellers, songwriters, and visionaries.

In its shadow are all of the complexes that display mental imbalance, delusion, deception, and dyslexia.

Mercury And Pluto

Mercury Pluto brings the most penetrating and insightful ability to the mind. These natives are able to relentlessly dive into a subject to its core or totally ignore that which is perceived as simply superficial.

In its shadow these natives can be mentally controlling and intellectually overwhelming. They are great investigators and researchers. Its shadow holds obsessions and deep-seated phobia that distort their perception and color their ideas and opinions.

Seeing The Bigger Picture

[This is a reference to the archetype of Pallas Athene, the "octave transformer" between Mercury and Uranus discussed in the next chapter. "The Discovery of the Outer Planets & Asteroids]

It is important to remember that we should not make the assumption that all facilitating aspects by definition are "good" or that challenging aspects are all inherently "bad".

The challenges and crises that occur during our lifetime are the catalysts for personal growth. It is not what happens that makes it good or bad, it is how we react or respond to the event.
An astrologer who has been professionally trained has the toolset to objectively interpret a birth chart and the current celestial influences acting on it.

It is most important to recognize that the stars and planets do not control us, they merely reflect us. The space in which Mercury operates is liminal space. Mercury opens the threshold between "what is not any longer" and "what is not yet". This vortex is saturated with potentiality, even as it seems to not contain anything that seems real.

Wherever Mercury is, wherever he resides in a chart, is a threshold. It is the space of mental construction and intention. In this role Mercury acts as the incubator of who we are becoming.

When Gemini thoughts polarize as Sagittarian beliefs and are synthesized with the meaning and values correlating to Venus/Aphrodite, the resulting priorities being handed off to Mars for execution, thoughts become words, words become actions, and actions become deeds.

> Your words become your actions,
> Your actions become your habits. Your habits become your

values,
Your values become your destiny.
-- Mahatma Gandhi

References:

Edis, Freda, The God Between: A Study of Astrological Mercury, Arkana, 1996.

Lachman, Gary, The Quest for Hermes Trismegistus: From Egypt to the Modern World", Floris Books, 2011.

Clark, Brian, The Sibling Constellation, Arkana/Penguin Books, 1999

Copenhaver, Brian P., Hermetica: the Greek Corpus Hermeticum and the Latin Asclepius in a new English translation, Cambridge University Press, Oct 12, 1995.

Green, Jeffrey, "The Nature and Function of Mercury and Its Archetypal Role in Consciousness" http://schoolofevolutionaryastrology.com/school/wp-content/uploads/Mercury_Article.pdf
Rudhyar, Dane, "An Astrological Study of Psychological Complexes", http://www.khaldea.com/rudhyar/aspc/.

Meyer, Michael R., "The 4 Faces of Mercury", http://khaldea.com/planets/merc_type.shtml.

Sasportas , Howard, The Inner Planets: The Building Blocks of Personal Reality, Weiser Books, Jan 15, 1993.

The Kybailion, Three Iniatiates to Hermes TrisMegistus (1908),
Health Research, Southgate Publishers, 1970.

Homer, The Odyssey, translated by Robert Fables, Penguin Books, New York, 1997, Book 5:47.

http://khaldea.com

http://www.theoi.com

https://symbolreader.net

THE DISCOVERY OF THE OUTER PLANETS & ASTEROIDS: ASTROLOGY & MYTHOLOGY

U p until the time of the American and French Revolutions, the only known 7 planets were those visible to the naked eye. The most distant of these was Saturn, who with his "ring pass not" was considered to be the outermost boundary of the solar system.

All of the planets except Venus (Aphrodite) and the Moon, which is not a planet, were male sky gods ~Mercury (Hermes), Mars (Ares), Jupiter (Zeus), and Saturn (Kronos). In 1781 Uranus was discovered by William Herschel with astonishing accuracy, using Bode's Law, a mathematical equation calculated in 1771.

> "Bode's Law is a mathematical hypothesis that the bodies in some orbital systems, including the Sun's, orbit at semi-major axes in a function of planetary sequence. The formula suggests that, extending outward, each planet would be approximately twice as far from the Sun as the one before. The hypothesis correctly anticipated the orbits of Ceres (in the asteroid belt) and Uranus, but failed as a predictor of Neptune's orbit." --https://en.wikipedia.org/wiki/Titius–Bode_law

Discoveries of new celestial bodies coincide with quantum leaps in human consciousness. There is a direct correlation between the celestial energetic matrix and human consciousness ~ As Above, So Below.

We are in the place between primordial Gaia~Earth and Ouranos~Sky and stand as an equal part of both. The Earth and the Solar System are complete universes. Each is a complete self sustaining system. We also are a complete mind=body=spirit biophysical universe.

The Discovery Of Uranus

All of the planets within Saturn's orbit represent the subjective components of the human psyche, for instance and admittedly oversimplified, how we think, how we love, how we behave, and so on.

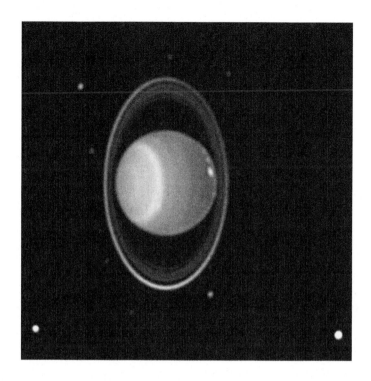

Uranus was the first planet observed beyond Saturn. The planets beyond Saturn are transpersonal, representing both the collective unconscious and individuated unconscious that lie below the surface of our awareness. Their archetypes are not personal like the inner planets, Mercury, Venus, and Mars. They are bigger than ourselves. The outer planets are expanding human conscious by:

○ Activating our highest human potentials

○ Expanding our awareness to that which is greater than ourselves

○ Allowing us to see "beyond the Veil" ~ reconnect to All-That-Is

○ Generating greater awareness of our evolutionary process

The discovery of Uranus was truly revolutionary. First sighted around the time of the American and French Revolutions, the discovery of Uranus changed everything. Uranus represents the dynamic in human consciousness that initiates the process of individuation, which awakens the Soul's deep memory of its connection to reality in a broader collective context.

Richard Tarnas defines the nature of Uranus as Promethean. Uranus is progressive and forward looking. He is the planet of liberation and revolution. His mission is cultural de-conditioning. Uranus interrupts, disrupts, and deconstructs consensus reality.

Remarkably, Uranus was not only observed to be a ringed planet, it was also observed to be spinning on its side and backwards, declaring its fundamental intention to de-condition what we think we know.

The Discovery Of Neptune

The map of the heavens has expanded as the human consciousness has expanded. The following century, Neptune was discovered in 1846, however Bode's Law failed to predict its orbit.

Two days before the discovery of Neptune, The Virgin Mary is said to have appeared to two children in La Salette, France.

> "On the evening of Saturday, 19 September 1846, Maximin Giraud and Melanie Calvat (called Mathieu) returned from the mountain where they had been minding cows and reported seeing "a beautiful lady" on Mount Sous-Les Baisses, weeping bitterly. They described her as sitting with her elbows resting on her knees and her face buried in her hands. She was clothed in a white robe studded with pearls; and a gold colored apron; white shoes and roses about her feet and high headdress. Around her neck she wore a crucifix suspended from a small chain.
>
> According to their account, she continued to weep even as she

spoke to them, first in French, then in their own dialect of Occitan. After giving a secret to each child, the apparition walked up a hill and vanished."

https://en.wikipedia.org/wiki/Our_Lady_of_La_Salette.

Neptune was actually first observed by Galileo in 1613.

> "John Herschel almost discovered Neptune the same way his father, William Herschel had discovered Uranus in 1781, by chance observation. In an 1846 letter to Wilhelm Struve, John Herschel states that he observed Neptune during a sweep of the sky on July 14, 1830. Although his telescope was powerful enough to resolve Neptune into a small blue disk and show it to be a planet, he did not recognize it at the time and mistook it for a star." --Gunther Buttmann. The Shadow of the Telescope: a biography of John Herschel. James Clarke and Co.

As the planet of consciousness itself, Neptune awakens and reveals the dimensions of reality that exist outside of Time and Space. Neptune dissolves the Veil that conceals the true nature of reality. Neptune dissolves anything and everything that stands between the subjective ego and The-Source-of-All-That-Is, enabling a reconnection.

The Discovery Of Pluto

Pluto came into awareness with the advent of the Atomic Age, the tremendous power of the atom, and the destructive weaponry derived from it. The discovery of Pluto in 1930 was also not found using Bode's law, however it was roughly at the position the law had predicted for Neptune.

Since the 1930s the world has been transformed. The impact of seeming localized events are now globalized. Technology has synthesized planetary timezones. World unification is birthing, albeit with disparity and conflict.

The Sky Goddesses

In 1596, Johannes Kepler predicted,

> "Between Mars and Jupiter, I place a planet ".

No planet was found there. However, in 1801, Giuseppe Piazzi, an Italian astronomer discovered what we now know as the dwarf planet Ceres, orbiting between Jupiter and Mars, in the exact place that Kepler predicted!

Piazzi named this newly discovered asteroid, Ceres because Piazzi's observatory was located in the place where legend says that Pluto abducted Persephone, daughter of Ceres, Demeter to the Greeks. Ceres was reclassified as a dwarf planet, when Pluto was reclassified, also to a dwarf planet. Many astrologers strongly disagree with this reduction of Pluto's importance.

> "When a certain celestial body is prominent in the sky at the time of your birth, the mythic biography of that deity contributes a shaping influence upon the course of your life and your destiny". http://www.demetrageorge.com/Mythology_Foundation_Astrology.pdf

There are over 400,000 known asteroids in the asteroid belt between Mars and Jupiter. Around 15,000 of them have been named and mapped.

The most commonly used asteroids in astrological consultations are the three sisters of Jupiter (Zeus)-- Ceres (Demeter), Juno (Hera), Vesta (Hestia), and Pallas Athene (Minerva), born parthenogenetically from the crown chakra of Zeus.

Pallas Athene was subsequently discovered in 1802, Juno in 1804, and Vesta in 1807 ~ all in the asteroid belt between Mars and Jupiter.

Over a century later in 1973, with the publication of <u>Epheme-</u><u>rides of the Asteroids: Ceres, Pallas, Juno, Vesta, 1900-2000</u>, by Eleanor Bach and George Climlas, the application and importance of asteroids came into increasingly widespread usage by the astrological community.

Each of these new sky goddesses represents a previously unexpressed astrological component of the feminine archetype. They also evidence how over time patriarchy had increased it hold on the belief systems of the classical ages. The expression of the feminine archetype became increasingly fragmented into the multiple goddesses of the Greek and Roman pantheons.

The Divine Mother

> "Once upon a time, the many cultures of this world were all part of the gynocratic age. Paternity had not yet been discovered, and it was thought "... that women bore fruit like trees--when they were ripe. Childbirth was mysterious. It was vital. And it was envied. Women were worshipped because of it, were considered superior because of it Men were on the periphery. The discovery of paternity, of sexual cause and childbirth effect, was cataclysmic for society".
>
> --Introduction by Gloria Steinem, Wonder Woman Interpretive essay by Phyllis Chesler

We know the Divine Mother in her un-manifested entirety as the Yin principle. She is receptive, dark, moist, passive, cold, soft, and yielding.

To the Greeks she appears first as primordial Nyx, Night. Nyx mated with Chaos and bore Erebus, Darkness. Night mated with Darkness and bore Aether, Light and Air, and Hemera, Day. Night gives birth to Day at dawn and retrieves it at dusk. Night and

Chaos existed before time or space.

Our world suffers from being overwhelmed by solar experience. Most metropolitan areas never achieve complete darkness because of all the 24 hour ambient lighting. Diurnal rhythm lulls us into sleep each night. Nyx is hidden from us. We are only able to reach Night through her children Hypnos, Sleep and Oneiroi, Dreams. In our world today, we are blinded by the light of day. We have lost the night.

Goddesses Of The Fertile Crescent

The earliest known ancient spiritual traditions such as those practiced in Egypt, Sumer and Babylonia were centered on the sacredness of birth and procreation. Nut, Ishtar, Astarte, and Inanna were expressions of the totality of sensuality and sexuality of the feminine archetype.

Sexuality was sacred and there were rites and temples dedicated to it. Childbirth was considered to be the most mysterious and sacred event in human experience.

Matriarchy however, did not mean the rule of women. When the recognition came that men played a role in the birth process, the matriarchal tradition was soon overtaken by patriarchal governance.

The Greek And Roman Pantheons

The Greeks and Roman pantheons were polytheistic. Their pantheons included both male and female deities. The patriarchal posture of Greeks cosmology fragmented the feminine archetype into separate parts. This leads to a gradual dilution of the singularity of the feminine expression.

Botticelli "Primavera

Ishtar became Aprhrodite, Ceres, Pallas, Vesta, Juno, and Diana and all the other goddesses. They were also demonized as Hecate, the Moirai, Lilith, and Eve. Gradually over time, the male sky gods ascended: Mercury, Mars, Saturn, Uranus, Saturn, Jupiter, Neptune, and Pluto.

The Repression Of Sexuality In The Middle Ages

Out of the need to counter the influence of the sexually exuberant pagan cultures migrating from the north, throughout the Middle Ages the Church of Rome further subverted the feminine archetype.

Doctrines established religious dogma that vilified the libidinous, shamanic traditions inherent in indigenous, pagan culture, as the clerics ecclesiastically severed spirit from flesh.
In order to create a new status quo, gnosis, the knowledge of spiritual mysteries, was hidden on a scale equal only to the

burning of the Library at Alexandria.

Venus Aphrodite

"Wall painting in the House of Venus in the Shell in Pompeii"

Venus was the complete form of the relationship goddess in Roman mythology. She was Aphrodite to the Greeks. Venus/Aphrodite is the ultimate expression of beauty, sexuality, and personal magnetism. Her archetype spans the range of experience of relationship.

Venus is said to rule 2 signs of the zodiac. The Yin, inner expression of Venus is through her rulership of
Taurus. In the natural zodiac, Taurus is the ruler of the 2nd House. As such, Taurus correlates to our essential resources, and our own self-worth. Taurus correlates to what we value and consider indispensable. As such it is about procreation of the species.

As her outer, Yang expression, Venus rules the sign of Libra. She is the conduit between self and others, or as Martin Buber stated it, "I and Thou". Venus becomes the mirror to our own inner being as our light is and shadow is projected onto others.

Venus correlates astrologically to magnetism. The value we place on ourselves becomes the magnetic frequency we project onto all of our relationships with others. These are the people who will show up in the 7th House. It will also be reflected in what we attract in the 8th House, either as a proactive or as cataclysmic learning experience.

An Asteroid Mandala

In "Asteroid Goddesses", Demetra George and Douglas Bloch describe the relationship between the Moon, Venus, and the 4 asteroids, as a mandala.

As the expression of the Yin principle, the Moon occupies the entire field of the mandala. As the complete archetype of feminine sexuality, Venus Aphrodite holds the center of this energetic template. Four asteroids, Ceres, Juno, Vesta, and Pallas Athene occupy the angles, each representing a component of the entire feminine archetype.

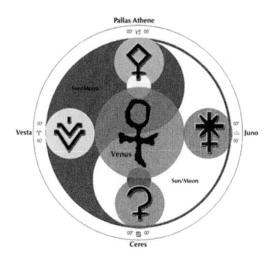

Ceres who correlates to motherhood and the parental bond anchors the Inum Coeli at the 4th house cusp.

> "CERES – the mother, the feminine appears as Ceres representing her procreative aspect as mother in her propagation and nurturing of the species. Ceres represents the mothering function within the human psyche which expresses in BOTH men

and women. Women and men also have a fathering function, symbolized by Saturn. To the extent that these human (masculine and feminine) functions have polarized in sexual role stereotyping, women have largely expressed only Ceres (as mother) and projected Saturn. Likewise, men have only expressed Saturn (as father) and projected Ceres."
--Demetra George, Asteroid Goddesses

Pallas Athene, Goddess of realized accomplishment, stands proudly at the Medium Coeli ~ the 10th house cusp.

Vesta, Guardian of the Sacred Fire, the sister who is bound to no man, but has aspired to a sacred bond with her authentic self, actualizes at the Ascendant.

> "VESTA – the sister, representing the self-containment of the feminine nature as Virgin and sister, complete in-one-self, belonging to no man. Although Vesta interacts with the masculine, she remains autonomous and becomes reabsorbed back into herself. More involved with individual accomplishment."
> --Demetra George, Asteroid Goddesses

Juno, the faithful committed wife, resides on the Descendant.

> "JUNO – the wife, representing the union of the feminine nature with the masculine as consort and wife through Sacred Marriage, Conjunctio. Juno unifies with the masculine principle. The symbolic union completes the circle of the mandala of feminine expression. Women have largely manifested the emotional commitment and caretaking of the partnership relationship symbolized by Juno, leaving the men more of the outer world expressions denoted by the Sun and Jupiter. For men, the activation of these centers makes it increasingly difficult to continue to repress or project their feminine aspects. The resolution of these challenges lies in transforming personal power into mutual trust and fusion. Learning to forgive oneself and one's partner will bring about the much-needed healing." -- Demetra George, Asteroid Goddesses

These asteroids do not assert rulership of these houses. There is however, an archetypal synchronicity with each of those place-ments.

Ceres, Goddess of Agriculture, is related to Earth. Pallas Athene, Warrior Goddess of Wisdom is a Air. Juno is Water. Vesta is Fire.

Each of these asteroids has significations and keywords, just as the archetypes representing the planets and signs. Asteroid archetypes covers a broad spectrum of expression, and when the story is retold, the nuances, variations, and synchronicities emerge.

In my work, I have found that the stories the mythology holds opens the space for the gifts of the night, intuition and dreams, to come in.

> "Myth is an attempt to narrate a whole human experience, of which the purpose is too deep, going too deep in the blood and soul, for mental explanation or description." --D.H. Lawrence Apocalypse

Persephone

The myth of Ceres/Demeter is very revealing when overlaid on the context of a natal chart. All depth psychology modalities seem to agree on one thing: that our early childhood sets up the nature of the psychological and emotional framework for the lifetime. How we were nurtured, or not, prescribes the timbre of our emotional register through life.

Ceres, Demeter to the Greeks, was the Goddess of Agriculture and along with her daughter Persephone, the Goddess of Spring Growth. Persephone, whose name could not be uttered, was also called Kore, the Maiden.They were the iconic mother daughter relationship. Together they roamed the hills, valleys, and fields spreading fertility and abundance.

Demeter, Zeus, and Hades were siblings. Hades had fallen in love with Persphone. Unbeknownst to Demeter, Hades asked Zeus for Persephone, and Zeus agreed.

One day while Persephone was lost in reverie picking Narcissus, Hades, wearing his helmet of invisibility, came charging up in his chariot from his Underworld kingdom. He abducted Persephone and took her back down to his unseen world as his bride.

By some accounts Persephone surrendered willingly to Hades as his bride. The story of her being carried off by Hades/Pluto, against her will, is not mentioned by Homer, who simply describes her as his wife and queen Her abduction is first mentioned by Hesiod (Theog. 914).

Zeus, it is said, advised Pluto, who was in love with the beautiful Persephone, to carry her off, as her mother, Demeter, was not likely to allow her daughter to go down to Hades. Pluto accordingly carried her off while she was gathering flowers with Artemis and Athena.

Is the story of the rape a patriarchal distortion? Regardless of how the loss occurred, Demeter was in deep despair for the disappearance of her beloved daughter. Apollo came to her and told her what happened. He told her that he knew that Hecate had witnessed the event. Hecate told Demeter what had transpired. With Hekate holding her torches aloft, together they searched the world high and low.

In another version, Hekate said that she heard the event, but did not see it, but she knew that Apollo had seen it. Demeter went to Apollo who told her what had taken place.

When she understood that her brothers had conspired against her and stolen her daughter, Demeter was furious. She went to Zeus and asked him to rescind his agreement with Hades. Zeus refused. Her daughter was gone down into the Underworld and she believed that her brothers were responsible. The personal loss and heartbreak was unbearable. Demeter threatened to blight the land, to cause all of the crops in the fields to wither and die and bring famine to mankind. In one version of the story she acted on her threat.

Faced with a peril that if mankind starved there would be no one to worship him, Zeus had no choice but to relinquish. He sent Hermes, the only God who could enter the Underworld without harm, to retrieve Persephone.

All during her captivity, Persephone had refused to eat. When Hades told her that she would be released, he offered her a pomegranate seed, a talisman of conjugal union, which she tasted, binding her to spend a portion of the year in the Underworld with her husband Hades.

She would then return to the world above for a time, creating the cycle of the seasons.

By some accounts Persephone fully embraced her role as Queen of the Underworld. The myth has a variety of different meanings.

Birth and death and the resulting loss and grief.
The parental bond.

Attachment and the loss resulting from over-attachment.

The nature of our relationship to our parents, and to our children as their parents. How we were nurtured. How we nurture our children and others.

The loss of a child, or the loss of someone or something that we have become deeply, or overly attached to.

Sexual abuse from a family member.

"Green thumb" and the ability to nurture as a farmer or gardener.

Eating disorders.

Eleusinian Mysteries

The Eleusinian Mysteries were secret religious rites practiced at Eleusis in Ancient Greece. The mysteries centered around Demeter, Persephone, and Triptolemas, a child Demeter tried to make immortal as a surrogate for her lost child. The rites honored Persephone (Kore) as both the Goddess of Spring, and the Queen of the Lower World. In the mysteries, the return of Kore from the Underworld was regarded as the symbol of immortality.

Asteroids In The Birth Chart

> "The emergence of the asteroids also coincides with the awakening of new centers of awareness in the evolution of consciousness. The first four sighted, named after great goddesses of antiquity – Ceres, Pallas, Vesta, Juno – represent a rediscovery and renewed strengthening of the feminine principles in the collective psyche. As the vibratory rate of the feminine polarity in the energy field of the physical world has intensified, new issues concerning feminine and masculine roles and functioning are affecting women, men, and society as a whole."
> — Demetra George, Asteroid Goddesses

Asteroids are not planets. They are however important supporting actors. Asteroids provide a richer and fuller meaning to a birth chart. They hold powerful feminine energies that cannot be expressed by the male sky gods, Mars, Saturn, Uranus, Neptune, and Pluto. They bring additional insights, depth, and dimension. Their specific meanings connect with and highlight other identified chart themes and signatures. Each of the asteroids besides Ceres has an equally compelling mythology.

Pallas Athene, Goddess of Wisdom, was born parthenogenetically from her father Zeus's crown chakra. She was fully clad in golden armor, holding her spear shield and waving her spear high in the air, shouting a battle cry.

Resisting the advances of all men, Pallas Athene was virginal like Artemis. As the Goddess of Wisdom she breeds mental progeny. She informs with her strategies by showing us the big picture. When we grasp the whole design, we can understand where all the smaller pieces fit together. She is the archetype of the civic-minded activist, patron of the arts, androgynous woman who stands in her power equally with men ~ a woman in a man's world.

Vesta/Hestia brings us into sacred union with ourselves. She represents the search for the authentic self, and our commitment to the ideals that define us. Dedicated to a sacred communal life, the Vestals were tasked with the oversight and protection of the communal fire. She is the only goddess who has no public temple. Her temple was in the hearth in each home where she resided, in the home fire that burned individually and collectively.

Not virgins, only unmarried women by Roman custom and parlance. Their sacred bond was to themselves, their sacred community and the shared work.

The Greek and Roman Empires were military cultures, often at war. It has also been suggested that they provided service that encouraged the re-entry into society of soldiers returning home from war.

Juno/Hera as the faithful wife exemplifies our commitment to relationship as well as the emotional roller coaster experience it sometimes brings. She was of equal status to her husband Zeus, but she was marginalized.

Cycles of power and revenge in relationships

Contracts with others

Issues around fidelity

Codependency

Beauty and adornment

Their archetypes can also be active in a man's chart as well.

Men are fathers and have relationships to their parents and children.

They can also have creative inspiration (Pallas)

Be committed to a connection to their authentic self (Vesta)

Desire to be faithfully committed partners (Juno)

"The feminine principle manifests in both men and women. Feminine is NOT a synonym for female or woman, but indicates one half of a human polarity – and neither half, masculine or feminine, exists without the other. Both sides exist within both human sexes." While in the past the feminine principle has been expressed primarily by women, due to the present rebalancing of masculine and feminine energies signified by the emergence of the asteroids, the men are now identifying and expressing their feminine nature."
—Demetra George, Asteroid Goddesses

According to Jennifer Barker Woolger, in "The Goddess Within", the goddess asteroids in a man's chart can also reveal the type of woman to whom they will be attracted.

It is important to note that not every asteroid is significant in every chart. Their significance depends on their prominence by angularity and aspect to other prominent planets and lights.The Women's Movement

Since the discovery of Ceres and her sisters in the late 19th Century, we have witnessed a steady re-emergence of the matriarchy into our culture. Here is a timeline of some of the significant advances in the last century:

The Suffragette movement in the US and in the UK in the late 19th Century was the turning point of the return of the Matriarchy

1919: The 19th Amendment was passed granting women the right to vote

1923: Margaret Sanger opened the first birth control clinic in New York City.

1932:Amelia Earhart makes the first solo flight by a woman across the Atlantic.
1955: Rosa Parks is arrested in Montgomery, Alabama, for refusing to give up her seat on a bus to a white man, thus sparking the U.S. civil rights movement.

1963: Betty Friedan published The Feminine Mystique, which galvanizes the women's rights movement.

1964: Title VII of the Civil Rights Act prohibits discrimination in employment on the basis of race or sex.

1965:, a Supreme Court ruling (Griswold v. Connecticut) legalizes birth control for married couples in the United States.

1973: Roe v. Wade -- the Supreme Court upheld legalized abortion

1981: Sandra Day O'Connor is the first woman on the U.S. Supreme Court

1984: Geraldine Ferraro becomes the first woman nominated for vice president by a major party

2007: Nancy Pelosi is sworn in as the first female speaker of the U.S. House of Representatives

2008: Hillary Rodham Clinton is the first woman to become a leading candidate for a presidential nomination

2016: Hillary Rodham Clinton becomes the first woman to be a candidate for POTUS.

2020: Ruth Bader Ginsberg becomes the 1st woman to lay in state the Capital Rotunda .

There has been an equally profound effect on the lives of men. We have seen a wider rejection of the macho stereotype. Men are performing traditional female roles as secretaries, nurses, and househusbands.   Men are sharing the responsibilities of raising children.   Courts are increasingly awarding child cus-tody to men, and many more single male parents are adopting children.

"Sandra" ~ A Case Study

I would like to refer to a case study of someone who came to me for a consultation. I will call her "Sandra".

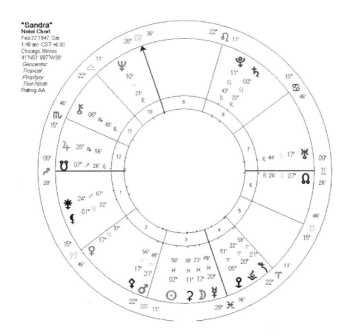

In Sandra's chart:

Pluto in Leo in the her 8th House is conjunct Saturn.
Pluto sextiles Neptune in Libra in the 10th House.
Pluto and Neptune form a Yod, or Finger of God configuration with Ceres in Pisces in the 3rd House ~ Ceres being the focal point of the Yod.
Ceres is conjunct the Moon, also in Pisces.
12th House Jupiter in Scorpio is the ruler of the chart
12th House South Node in Sagittarius conjunct the Ascendant.
12th House Jupiter in Scorpio is the ruler of the Lunar South Node
Jupiter squares the 3rd House Pisces Sun.

Jupiter squares 2nd House Mars in Aquarius
Jupiter trines Mercury in Pisces 3rd.

The Yod formation between Ceres, Neptune, and Pluto brought Sandra into a birth family situation where she felt isolated and her emotional nature was repressed and denied. Sandra was adopted. She was born feeling alone and abandoned from birth. Her the environment of her adoptive family lacked any parental nurturing or emotional support.

In her own words, Sandra describes her early childhood,

> "I was adopted at the age of two weeks. My father was an unemotional stern German man "...we were like oil and water as I was sensitive and emotional. Showing emotion was a big no-no in the family. My Mom"...knew her role as mother"...she was passive "...and bowed to my Dad's needs. She was unable to bear children. My Dad arranged through an attorney to adopt two kids"...I felt like an alien in the family"

Sandra has been working on the themes of her sense of isolation, of having her power taken away, and the recurring traumas of betrayal and abandonment (Pluto Leo 8th square Chiron Scorpio 11th).

She has found the courage to explore her own truth in the world outside her family (Sagittarius SN conjunct Ascendant) though it has been hard to overcome the pain and sensitivity she carries as karmic experience, and to be able to stand in her own power (Jupiter Scorpio square Sun Pisces).

She still feels a deep rage against those who betrayed and abused her. (Jupiter Scorpio square Mars Aquarius)

Her evolutionary intentions via her Pluto polarity point in Aquarius 2nd House are to develop her own inner resources and strength, to become her own father; to take responsibility for herself in this lifetime. (Capricorn 2nd, Saturn Leo 8th)

We can clearly see how Ceres reflects the Soul's unfinished business via Sandra's birth family environment and how it adds depth to the detail of those early years, which set the emotional backdrop of the entire lifetime.

So, What Is The State Of The "Rebirth Of The Divine Feminine"?

Five years ago this appeared in the web addition of The Huffington Post:

> "Despite great strides made by the international women's rights movement over many years, women and girls around the world are still married as children or trafficked into forced labor and sex slavery. They are refused access to education and political participation, and some are trapped in conflicts where rape is perpetrated as a weapon of war. Around the world, deaths related to pregnancy and childbirth are needlessly high, and women are prevented from making deeply personal choices in their private lives." http://www.huffington-post.com/2014/04/09/paycheck-fairness-act_n_5118254.html 10)

The rebirth of the Divine Feminine is about the balance of the anima and the animus ~ Transcending Duality to create Unity. It is about the recognition of the sanctity of life, the sacredness of birth, and the mystery of death.
It is about our reconnection to the sacredness of the natural world and all living things. It is the desire and intention to find equality and balance in all things.

We do not come into this world with tabula rasa, as the rationalists would have us believe. Our "slate" is richly notated, foot marked and cross-referenced.

> "An archetype is like an old watercourse along which the water of life has flowed for centuries, digging a deep channel for itself.

The longer it has flowed in this channel the more likely it is that sooner or later the water will return to its old bed." --Carl Jung "Civilization in Transition"

These archetypes live on within us, buried deep in the "underground" of our Uranian individuated unconscious. The circumstances and relationships that our Soul has aligned for us are designed to reveal those parts of us that we cannot see. Mythology holds the template, the image of those archetypes. The wisdom has been preserved for centuries, hidden by those who would erase it, protected for those who would seek to find it. Astrology shows the way these universal archetypes are unfolding on our paths backwards and forwards through this present moment.

References

https://en.wikipedia.org/wiki/Our_Lady_of_La_Salette

Gunther Buttmann. The Shadow of the Telescope: a biography of John Herschel. James Clarke and Co.

Johannes Kepler Mysterium Cosmographicum

http://www.demetrageorge.com/Mythology_Foundation_Astrology.pdf

Introduction by Gloria Steinem, Wonder Woman Interpretive essay by Phyllis Chesler

Demetra George and Douglas Bloch, Asteroid Goddesses

D.H. Lawrence Apocalypse
https://www.theoi.com/Khthonios/Persephone.html
ttp://www.huffingtonpost.com/2014/04/09/paycheck-fairness-act_n_5118254.html

Civilization in Transition, Carl Jung

THE WATER TRIAD: THE EVOLUTION
OF CONSCIOUSNESS

T he evolution of consciousness, and its growth and development in human experience can be understood through the study of the Water element.

All of Creation is conscious -- minerals, plants, animals, and of course human beings.

Consciousness is like water. It fills up every space it passes through. Like water, the structure of consciousness is determined by the nature of the structure it occupies.

What Is The Nature Of Consciousness?

Plants eat minerals, and we eat the plants. Minerals and plants are both our food and our medicine. Minerals and (Splants are here unconditionally to support us, and they wait patiently for us to ask for their help.

Gemstones have been sought after since earliest recorded history, not just for their beauty, but for their inherent energetic properties.

Indigenous cultures throughout history have recognized the healing properties of sacred plants.

Animals are also here to support our well-being. They have been our working partners for millennia. Many sacrifice themselves for our sustenance. They are here as our companions. To some of us they are an important member of our family.

The consciousness of minerals is determined by the nature of the mineral. The consciousness of plants is determined by the nature of the plant. The consciousness of animals is determined by the nature of the animal. Human consciousness is determined by the nature of human experience.

Mineral and plant consciousness is a non-reasoning, adaptively instinctive property. Behavior is survival oriented.

Animals do exhibit behavior that suggests a higher level of being--an intelligence capable of logical reasoning learned through direct emotional experience.

There is however Hindu teaching that posits the idea that only Man can know God. Perhaps this remains just an idea, which we might not be able to prove or disprove.

The Water Signs

From an astrological perspective we can gain an understanding of the dynamics of human consciousness through the study of Water element triad

Moon/Cancer/4th House
Pluto/Scorpio/8th House
Neptune/Pisces/12th House

The archetype of Pisces and Neptune express in the context that correlats to All-That-Is, Creation/Creator, the Zero Point Field, Source, God/ess. This archetype can be described as The Ocean.

So"...what is the nature of the ocean? The ocean contains an infinite number of waves. The wave is the Soul. The ocean is Source.

Jeffrey Wolf Green asked the question,

"How can a perfect god create an imperfect world?"

The answer was that He/She is also evolving, perfectly imperfect, just like our world.

The Ocean (Source) contains an infinite number of Waves (Souls) within it. The ocean experiences itself through all of its waves. Each Soul has its own individual focus of consciousness, or ego.

Through the experiences of many lifetimes, the Soul also learns about itself. The Soul dreams itself into time and space in order to experience and grow. Each wave is a living dream. In that creative imagining, an illusion of separation is created.

Astrologically, Pluto, correlating to the wave and the Soul, carries the deepest security needs of the Soul, via its memory of all of its peak emotional experiences from the past.

The Soul has a dual desire nature. The first desire is the desire to separate from Source, in order to learn about itself through the full range of experiences of the 5 senses, in time and space. The Soul consciously pursues desire after desire hoping each accomplishment or acquisition will satisfy that deepest need for security--by pursuing money, career, relationship, power, and so on.

> "For reasons not always at the time explicable, there are specific occasions when events begin suddenly to take on a significance previously unsuspected; so that, before we really know where we are, life seems to have begun in earnest at last, and we ourselves, scarcely aware that any change has taken place, are careening uncontrollably down the slippery avenues of eternity."
> --Dancing to the Music of Time: First Movement, Anthony Powell

The second of the Soul's desires is the single desire to return to Source, which is finally realized after countless lifetimes of exhausting all of the other separating desires.

From lifetime to lifetime, we pick up where we left off. A single point of focus, a lens, so to speak is needed to be the point of interaction between inner and outer worlds. This is the egocentric structure that holds the emotional impressions from the past. The Moon correlates to the ego. Luna is our self image, how we see ourselves, because the Moon correlates to our emotional body.

The Moon is our conditioned self that contains the emotional history of all of the Soul's lifetimes. This is our refuge of emotional safety, our sanctuary. It is everything that is familiar to us, good and bad. The Moon is the tip of the Wave, our moment-to-moment interaction with our world, our inner guidance system.

Ego is not a bad word. If we did not have an ego, we would not know our own name. Like the lens on a movie projector we focus and navigate the world through our emotional body. Our emotions tell us when we are safe and when we are in danger.

The Soul's evolutionary journey can be charted through the trinity of the water signs. In Cancer and the 4th House we see ourselves for the first time--our self-image is formed, and we begin to develop a sense of who we are.

It is in Pluto and Scorpio's native 8th House that we realize that which we are not (yet). We become aware of our limitations and recognize those forces outside of ourselves that we are essential resources with which we are compelled to merge. This is Pluto driving the Soul's constant state of becoming.

In the 12th House, Pisces, Neptune's nativity, we literally find our true Self, as Neptune's magic works to dissolve anything and everything that stands between subjective ego and Soul ego. Pisces is the archetype that enables us to turn the corner away from all of the outer world distractions that are maintaining the illusion of separation. It is Neptune and Pisces that lead us finally to the realization, that we are not the wave. We have a body and mind, but that is not who we are. We are of and from Source and we finally arrive at the understanding that the only real and lasting security is through surrendering, accepting, and aligning consciously with Source

> "We can only learn to know ourselves and do what we can, namely, surrender our will and fulfill God's will in us."--Saint Teresa of Avila

ERIS: ASTROLOGY, ASTRONOMY
AND MYTHOLOGY

The Discovery Of Eris

In 2005, a team at the Palomar Observatory in Palo Alto, California, led by American astronomer Mike Brown reported the discovery of a planet orbiting in the Kuiper belt, out beyond the orbit of Neptune, a planet that was as large or larger than Pluto.

Eris and her moon Dysnomia
courtesy NASA, ESA, and M. Brown (California Institute of Technology)

Eris was first photographed on October 31, 2003, however, the object was so far away that its motion was not detected until it was reanalyzed on January 8, 2005, seen in an image that also revealed the presence of what would later be named Sedna.

The discovery of this contentious celestial body was destined to shake up both the world of astronomy and astrology alike. How can we but wonder at the synchronicity between the names assigned to the stars, planets, asteroids, and other celestial bodies, and the mythological counterparts and archetypes that they embody?

Following the discovery of the planet Neptune in 1846, there was considerable speculation that another planet might exist beyond its orbit. The search began in the middle of the 19th century and accelerated with the Percival Lowell's quest for Planet X.

In 1894, Percival Lowell founded the Lowell Observatory in Flagstaff, Arizona. Lowell's hypothesis was directed at explaining the apparent discrepancies in the orbits of the giant planets, particularly Uranus and Neptune. He postulated that the gravity of a large unseen planet could have disrupted the orbit of Uranus enough to account for the irregularities.

The first trans-Neptunian object to be discovered was Pluto in 1930. It took until 1992 to discover a second trans-Neptunian object orbiting the Sun directly, Albion.

The most massive TNO (trans-Neptunian object) known is Eris, followed by Pluto, 2007 OR10, Make-make and Haumea. More than 80 satellites have been discovered in orbit of trans-Neptunian objects. TNOs vary in color and are either grey-blue (BB) or very red (RR). They are thought to be composed of mixtures of rock, amorphous carbon and volatile ices such as water and methane, coated with tholins and other organic compounds.

Large Trans-Neptunian Objects (> 1000 km in Diameter) and Their Satellites

Eris was identified in images that had been captured a year earlier, but due to her extremely slow planetary speed, she had previously eluded detection. Around the same time, other transneptunian objects besides Eris, were discovered by Palomarbased team led by Brown: Sedna, Haumea, and Make-make. It was the discovery of Sedna that aided in the observation of Eris.

At the time of this writing, the 1st complete Jupiter cycle since the discovery of Eris has completed. Much information about this powerful new member of the celestial

pantheon has been observed and correlated in this relatively brief period of time.

What Is A Planet?

The word "planet" came to us by the ancient Greeks. In the Biblical and Classical Ages it was believed that the geocentric model that placed the Earth at the center of the universe, and everything in the sky, including the sky, revolved around it.

Greek astronomers used the term *asteres planetai*, "wandering stars", as the planets seemed as stars travel across the sky through the year. They called the motionless lights that were constant to each other, *asteres aplaneis*, the "fixed stars". This became the Greco-Roman pantheon. Hermes, Aphrodite, Ares, Zeus, and Kronos, became the visible 5 planets Mercury, Venus, Mars, Jupiter, and Saturn.

This Greco-Roman model persisted through the Middle Ages and until the late 18th Century, with the discovery of Uranus in 1781. However in all this time, from prehistory to the emergence of the modern world the only definition of the word "planet" rendered was "wanderer".

The five bodies currently called "planets" that were known to the Greeks were those visible to the naked eye: Mercury, Venus, Mars, Jupiter, and Saturn.

Observed to be about the same size as Pluto, Eris was initially considered to be a 10th planet. However, in consideration of the prospect of other TNOs of similar size being discovered in the future, motivated the International Astronomical Union (IAU) to define the term "planet" for the first time.

The asteroids had taken the vast majority of Greco-Roman names. Brown decided that because the object had been considered a planet for so long, it deserved a name from Greek or Roman mythology, like the other planets. Eris, whom Brown described as his favorite goddess, had fortunately escaped inclusion.

The name Eris was proposed and it was assigned following an unusually long period of time in which the object was known by the provisional designation 2003 UB.

There was uncertainty over whether the object would be classified as a planet or a minor planet. Different nomenclature procedures apply to these different classes of objects, so the decision on what to name the object had to wait for an International Astronomical Union ruling. As a result, for a time the object became known to the wider public as Xena.

"Xena" was an informal name used internally by the discovery team. It was inspired by the title character of the television series Xena: Warrior Princess. The discovery team had reportedly saved the nickname "Xena" for the first body they discovered that was larger than Pluto. According to Mike Brown, the naming was part of the effort to "get more female deities out there."

Because Eris was initially thought to be larger than Pluto, it was described as the "tenth planet" by NASA and in media reports of its discovery. In response to the uncertainty over its status, and because of ongoing debate over whether Pluto should be classified as a planet, the IAU delegated a group of astronomers to develop a sufficiently precise definition of the term planet to decide the issue.

This was announced as the IAU's Definition of a Planet in the Solar System, adopted on August 24, 2006.

The definition of a planet was adopted by the International Astronomical Union says a planet must do three things:

1. It must orbit a star (in our cosmic neighborhood, the Sun).

2. It must be big enough to have enough gravity to force it into a spherical shape.

3. It must be big enough that its gravity cleared away any other objects of a similar size near its orbit around the Sun.

Both Eris and Pluto were classified as dwarf planets, a category distinct from the new definition of planet. Under the IAU definition Eris became a "dwarf planet", along with Pluto ~ and in the case of Pluto, a classification that remains controversial.

At the same time, asteroid Ceres, with her almost perfectly round shape, was promoted in status and reclassified as a dwarf planet as well, along with Haumea, Make-make, and Sedna. The number of known planets in the Solar System reverted back to eight, the same as before Pluto's discovery in 1930.

Eris was born in controversy. The name reflects the discord in the astronomical community caused by the debate over the object's and Pluto's classification. With the dispute resolved, on September 13, 2006 the name Eris was finally accepted as the official name.

Planetary Characteristics

Eris is the most massive and second-largest dwarf planet known in the Solar System, and the ninth most massive object directly orbiting the Sun.

With the discovery of 2018 VG18, nicknamed "Farout" by its discovery team, Eris became the 2nd most distant observed Solar System object. At the time of this writing, it is also the largest object which has not yet been visited by a spacecraft.

Astronomers were finally able to accurately measure the diameter of the faraway dwarf planet Eris for the first time as it passed in front of a faint star, an event known as an occultation, in 2010 at the La Silla Observatory in Chile.

The observations show that Eris is an almost perfect twin of Pluto in size. Eris's mass is about 0.27% of the Earth mass, and about 27% more than dwarf planet Pluto, although Pluto is slightly larger by volume. The number 27 holds interesting significance evidenced in its dual appearance. It is also 33.

Eris is probably a large rocky body covered in a relatively thin mantle of ice. The surface of Eris was found to be extremely reflective, reflecting 96% of the light that falls on it. This is even brighter than fresh snow on Earth, making Eris one of the most reflective objects in the Solar System

Eris is about 3 times the distance from the Sun as Pluto. Eris has one known moon, Dysnomia, one of her mythical offspring, meaning Anarchy.

Because of her highly elliptical orbit, Eris spends approximately 20% of her 557-year orbit in the sign of Aries. The mean average transit through Aries, ruled by Mars lasts about 110 years.

This extended orbital period in Aries lends intensity and density to the relationships Eris has with Saturn, the traditional ruler, and Uranus, the modern ruler of Aquarius. The 84-year synodic cycle of Uranus permits 2 conjunctions each time Eris transits the sign of Aries. The 28-year cycle of Saturn permits 3 conjunctions.

The astronomy of Eris informs the astrology of Eris. Eris is very comfortable in the home of her brother Ares, God of War.

Who Is Eris?

Eris was born from the Nyx, Night, the primordial being that was the first to emerge from Chaos. She comes from the place that is deepest, darkest, and mostly invisible.

In "Theogony", Hesiod tells us,

> "Nyx bare hard-hearted Eris....abhorred Eris (Strife) bare painful Ponos (Toil), and Lethe (Forgetfulness), Limos (Starvation), the Algea (Pains), full of weeping, the Hysminai (Fightings), the Makhai (Battles), the Phonoi (Murders) and the Androkta-siai (Man-slaughters), the Neikea (Quarrels), the Pseudo-Logoi (Lies), the Amphilogiai (Disputes), Dysnomia (Lawlessness), and Ate (Ruin)"

Promordial Nyx (Night) was born from the Void, Chaos, Ain Soph. It was the Night that brought Eris, primordial strife and discord, sister to Desire (Eros), the Earth (Gaia), and the Abyss (Tartarus).

Also born from Nyx, were Moros (Doom), Ker (Violent Death), Thanatos (Death), Hypnos (Sleep), the tribe of Oneiroi (Dreams), Momos (Blame), Oizys (Misery), the Moirai (The Fates), Nemesis (Envy), Apate (Deceit), Philotes (Friendship), and Geras (Old Age), and the Hesperides (Nymphs of the West).

Hesiod also presents another perspective,

> "It was never true that there was only one Eris. There have always been two on earth. There is one you could like when you understand her. The other is hateful. The two Erites have separate natures. There is one Eris who builds up evil war, and slaughter. She is harsh; no man loves her, but under compulsion and by will of the immortals, men promote this rough Eris"

> "But the other one was born the elder daughter of black Nyx. Zeus, who sits on high and dwells in the bright air set her in the roots of the earth and among men; she is far kinder. She pushes the shiftless man to work, for all his laziness. A man looks at

his neighbour, who is rich: then he too wants work; for the rich man presses on with his ploughing and planting and ordering of his estate. So the neighbour envies the neighbour who presses on toward wealth. Such Eris is a good friend to mortals. —Hesiod "Works and Days"

In the Aeneid, Virgil describes Eris as

"maddening Discordia, her snaky locks entwined with bloody ribbons."

And Aeschylus,

"Eris is the last of the gods to close an argument."

Eris was the

"daimon of the strife of war, haunting the battlefield and delighting in human bloodshed.
—"https://www.theoi.com/Daimon/Eris.html

Most of what we know about the mythology of Eris can be found in the classics, in the writing of the Greek poets, Homer and Hesiod.

In "The Iliad", Homer connects Eris to the goddess of war,

"Enyo, sacker of cities"...Strife whose wrath is relentless, she is the sister and companion of murderous Ares, she who is only a little thing at the first, but thereafter grows until she strides on the earth with her head striking heaven. She then hurled down bitterness equally between both sides as she walked through the onslaught making men's pain heavier"...

Homer continues,

"Ares drove these the Trojans on, and the Akhaians greyeyed Athene, and Phobos (Terror) drove them, and Deimos (Fear)"...and Eris (Hate) whose wrath is relentless, she is the sister and companion of murderous Ares, she who is only a little thing at the first, but thereafter grows until she strides on the earth with her head striking heaven. She then hurled down bitterness equally between both sides as she walked through the onslaught making men's pain heavier the goddess Enyo, she carried with her the turmoil of shameless hatred

"Zeus sent down in speed to the fast ships of the Akhaians the wearisome goddess Eris, holding in her hands the portent of battle. She took her place on the huge-hollowed black ship of Odysseus which lay in the middle, so that she could cry out to both flanks . . .   There the goddess took her place, and cried out a great cry and terrible and loud, and put strength in all the Akhaians' hearts, to go on tirelessly with their fighting of battles."

The Golden Apple

Apples are abundant throughout culture and myth.

The forbidden fruit in the Garden of Eden.

An apple is responsible for Issac Newton's discovery of Gravity.

Snow White was put to sleep by an apple.

Johnny Appleseed was an American legend who introduced apple trees to large areas of the early United States.

Apple is the company that dreamed of placing a computer on every desk. (I am writing this on an Apple computer.)

This common fruit is embed in our language as well:

> The apple of my eye.
>
> American as apple pie.
>
> An apple a day keeps the doctor away.
>
> Comparing apples and oranges.
>
> Don't upset the apple cart.
>
> The apple never falls far from the tree.
>
> The "Big Apple"
>
> One rotten apple spoils the whole bunch.

And there is the famous apple that is blamed for the start of the Trojan War. The golden apples of Greek mythology grew in the sacred garden on the Western edge of Oceanus, tended by the Hesperides, the daughters of Nyx, Night. The tree that bears the auspicious fruit was the gift from Gaia to Hera upon her marriage to Zeus.

The story goes that Zeus planned a banquet in honor of the marriage of Peleus and Thetis, the future parents of Achilles. Chiron, who was tasked with sending out the invitations, snubbed Eris from the occasion thinking that her presence would be too offensive.

The Golden Apple of Discontent Jacob Jordaens

Eris showed up anyway, tossing a golden apple into the wedding party inscribed, "To the Fairest One" igniting a contest between Hera, Pallas Athena, and Aphrodite.
Paris, the son of Priam, King of Troy, was chosen to be the judge.

Each of the contestants offered Paris a prize. Hera promised him the Kingdoms of Europe and Asia. Pallas Athene offered him wisdom and skill in battle. It was Aphrodite however, who offered him Helen, daughter of Zeus, wife of Menelaus, King of Sparta, "the most beautiful woman in the world".

Peter Paul Rubens "The Judgement of Paris"

Aphrodite clothed herself with garments which the Kharites (Graces) and Horai (Seasons) had made for her and dyed in flowers of spring--such flowers as the Horai wear--in crocus and hyacinth and flourishing violet and the rose's lovely bloom, so sweet and delicious, and heavenly buds, the flowers of the narcissus and lily. In such perfumed garments is Aphrodite clothed at all seasons.

Then laughter-loving Aphrodite and her handmaidens wove sweet-smelling crowns of flowers of the earth and put them upon their heads--the bright-coiffed goddesses, the Nymphai and Kharites (Graces), and golden Aphrodite too, while they sang sweetly on the mount of many-fountained Ida. Beauty was the irresistible attraction. Paris chose Aphrodite, and abducted Helen, the wife of Menelaus, King of Sparta, and took her off to Troy.

Edward Poynter "Helen"

"Was this the face that launch'd a thousand ships,
and burnt the topless towers of Ilium?

To stop there would reduce Eris simply to being an instigator and not perhaps part of a team effort working towards transformation and transcendence.

The Trojan War which raged on for 10 years. When it was over, all of the great Greek and Trojan heroes of mythology were dead, save one, Aeneas, the son of Aphrodite and her lover Andhises, who is said to have sailed to Italy and founded the city of Rome. It not only marked the end of the Greek Classical Age, but the inception and emergence of the Roman Empire which would last for the next 1000 years.

A case could be made that it was Helen, not Eris, who is responsible for staring the Trojan War ~ Helen, "the face that launch'd a thousand ships, and burnt the topless towers of Ilium."

Myth suggests that Helen was not taken against her will. Neither is there any evidence that she ever expressed any remorse for her betrayal of Menelaus. With a truly sanguine sense of playfulness, she later taunted the Greek soldiers hidden within the Trojan Horse, tormenting them by cruelly mimicking the voices of their wives.

According to Euripides, Helen herself in fact never even got to Troy.

> "... a phantom was never to an alien prince's bed, wafted by wings of the oars I fled." (Helen to Menelaus. Euripides, Helen).

Euripides describes how Hermes brought Helen to Egypt, following Zeus' orders, while Paris sailed to Troy with a phantom fashioned by Hera. Helen lived in Egypt while Achaeans and Trojans slew each other at Troy.

The Astrology Of Eris

The astrology of Eris is still being observed and correlated, however a in very short period of time we have had the opportunity to witness the nature of her archetype up-close-and personal.

There is an unexplainable synchronicity between the naming of celestial bodies and their archetypal meaning. When first sighted, Eris was assigned the name Xena, correlating to the Warrior Princess, which was a popular television show around the time it was found. A year later she was renamed to conform to the Greco-Roman nomenclature for observed celestial bodies.

Eris is the grain of sand in the oyster that becomes an exquisite pearl. Chaos has the function of de-structuring what has become crystallized, allowing the creation of new form. Discomfort dislodges emotional inertia compelling action. When expressed peacefully as contrast, conflict can become unity where there was only duality. The divergent and separate become similar and connected.

There is an important synchronicity regarding the discovery of

Eris in the sign of Aries, the sign of the zodiac said to be ruled by Ares/Mars, The God of War. One version of the mythology tells us that Eris is the brother of Ares. Because of her highly elliptical orbit, Eris spends approximately 20% of her time in the single sign of Aries. Clearly she is very comfortable in her brother's house.

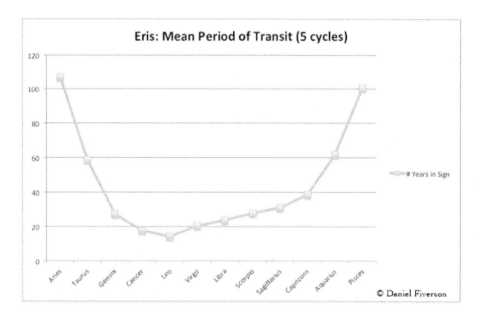

Aries is the Yang principle, energy moving outward from the center. It is Cardinal Fire, the first sign of the natural zodiac and the first of the Fire triad. Aries begins the process of self-actualization through elemental Fire, that completes as self-realization in Sagittarius.

Aries is the sign of the zodiac that correlates to initiation, and to birth itself. Aries correlates to the expression of pure instinct. There is little or no precognition. Action arises as the result of gut reaction, not measured response.

In the chart for her first sighting, the Lunar North Node was applying to a conjunction to Eris. The lunar nodes were also stationed. There is a suggestion of fate in the discovery. Mars in Sagittarius separates from a last quarter square to Uranus in Pisces. There is a forceful element of self-actualization in the archetypal intention.

Eris holds this archetype of an uncompromising urgency for resolution and delivers it through the deepest emotional portal that is available.

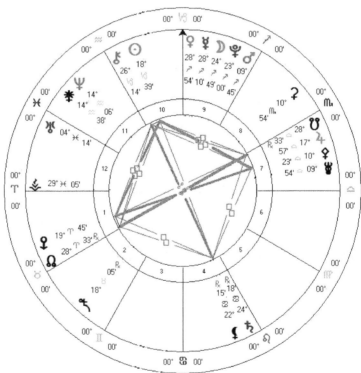

Eris identified
Event Chart
Jan 8 2005, Sat
12:00 pm PST +8:00
Palo Alto, CA
37°N26'31" 122°W08'31"
Geocentric
Tropical
0° Aries
True Node

At the time of her discovery, Eris was retrograde intensifying her influence. She retrogrades once a year. Because of her long transit of Aries, Eris stations at every degree in Aries. She lingers on each point *4 times,* maximizing the impact.

A Cardinal Grand Cross formed as Jupiter, conjunct the Lunar South Node opposed Eris. The Sun and Chiron in Capricorn opposed Saturn-Hygeia in Cancer, squaring the lunar nodes, Jupiter, and Eris. Chiron stands in a tight opposition to Saturn in Cancer maximizing potential for trauma and wounding. The 'astrological moment' is saturated with latent, unrealized, vital energy. There are tremendous tensions regarding the healing of ancient wounds.

A close trine from the Moon, Mercury, Venus, and Pluto in Sagittarius give Eris boundless opportunities for generating dramatic emotional displays of her disruptive prowess.

Uranus in Pisces challenges Eris. Life becomes theater, stranger than fiction. The Mars archetype is the expression of pure instinct; primal life force whose single necessity is self-actualization and self-expression. This moment is an initiation. It is the world of Self, which in its shadow sees all others merely the background to their own universe.

Greek Ares and Roman Mars are not identica archetypes. Mythologically, Ares expresses as blood lust, while Roman Mars shows up as a protector and guardian.
There is a numinous synchronicity between the naming of celestial bodies and their archetypal dynamics. I often wonder at the synchronistic connection between the planets and their divine counterparts, and how the planet correlates to one of the archetype's faces.

Eris is the grain of sand in the oyster that transforms into an exquisite pearl. Chaos has the function of de-structuring what has become crystallized, allowing space for the creation of new form. Discomfort dislodges emotional inertia, compelling action. When expressed peacefully as contrast, conflict can create unity where there was only duality. The divergent and separate become similar and connected.

Previous Transits Of Eris In Aries

Once every 500 years or so, the planet Uranus and dwarf planet Eris come together twice in the sign of Aries. Aries is the birth point, inception, Spirit into Matter. The helix of time returns to a starting point. A new Cosmic Cycle begins.

Because of her widely elliptical orbit, Eris spends with on average, 120 years in the sign of Aries. This makes perfect sense to me, as she is the brother of Ares, God of War, as she is very comfortable in her brother's home.

The last transit of Eris in Aries from 1392 to 1517 ushered in:

> The Spanish Inquisition
> 100 years of European war
> The discovery of the New World

The Spanish explorers brought with them warfare and the spread of Eurasian diseases which resulted in the genocide of the indigenous people of North and South America. Their mission was not humanitarian or scientific. Catholic priests whose mission was the systematicconversion of the natives and the eradication of their indigenous "primitive", pagan worship.

During this transit, Uranus conjoined Eris in Aries first in 1426 and then again in 1515. During these years,

> Across Europe, civil wars and economic dislocation were the legacies of the Hundred Years' War. The boundaries of sovereign dynastic domains were displaced or dissolved, fracturing the coagulated, patriarchal ascendancy of the Middle Ages, and opening the space for the new thought that was already birthing The Renaissance.

> Joan of Arc valiantly took up arms as a woman, to defend France from English occupation, in the end, losing her own life, yet canonized for her courage.

> The War of the Roses fractured Britain, as York and Lancaster battled for the English crown.

> Constantinople ~ the Capital of the known world since the end of the Roman Empire, falls to the Muslim Ottoman Turks, marking the end of the Byzantine Empire and the end of the Middle Ages.

> Johannes Gutenberg invented the printing press seeding the Renaissance.

The Medici's exerted their power and influence amid the emerging Renaissance as Florence became the center of the arts and learning.

Leonardo da Vinci created his masterworks.

Michelangelo painted the Sistine Chapel.

Martin Luther lists his 95 theses.

Copernicus publishes his theory that the Earth and the other planets revolve around the Sun.

The Church of England breaks away from the Roman Catholic Church.

Theresa of Avila was born.

In the years that followed,

The Spanish Inquisition sought to cleanse and purify religious expression and practice throughout Europe.

The Conquistadors explored Mexico and the American Southwest contributing to the genocide of the Native American population as a result of "Eurasian diseases such as influenza, bubonic plague and pneumonic plagues devastating the Native Americans who did not have immunity"

Current Transit Of Eris

Eris returned to the sign of Aries in 1922, after a 530 year hiatus. During each transit through Aries, Uranus meets up with Eris twice, 85 years apart. There were 3 conjunctions to Uranus in 1927 and 1928 at the very onset of the transit, precipitating the Wall Street Crash of 1929, the Great Depression, the rise of Adolf Hitler and Fascism and the outbreak of World War II.

We are currently in the culminating phase of this cycle. Uranus met up with Eris throughout 2015-2017 with another powerful self-actualizing, individuating, interruptive, and disruptive conjunction to Uranus. This conjunction occurred at the same time as the culminating phase of the 7 epic squares from Uranus to Pluto, which rocked the world beginning in 2012, as "what was too big to fail" began to crumble.

Over the decade, the number of random terrorist attacks, random gun violence and school shootings, political and economic polarization, ethnic and religious xenophobia, and undisguised hate crimes, and the virulent emergence of white supremacy. These transits also delivered the election of Donald Trump as President of the United States, an event that would leave a scar in US History.

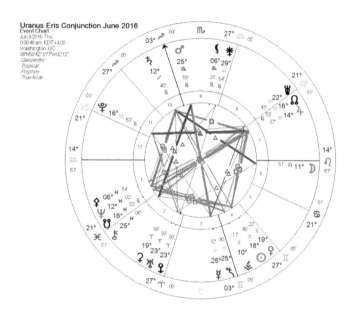

Last Quarter Square: Eris In Aries~Jupiter, Saturn, And Pluto

On January 16, 2020 Saturn in Capricorn formed a last quarter square to Eris in Aries for the last time this century. This particular transit will not occur again for over 500 years. The last quarter squares from these outer planets from CAPRICORN To ARIES are exceptionally rare. It will happen again until 2459-2519.

On January 26, 2020 an even rarer event occured..something that had not happened in 2700 years. Pluto in Capricorn perfected to a last quarter square to Eris in Aries.

The last time this occurred was in 691 BC. The last exact square between Pluto in Capricorn and Eris in Aries Pluto in Capricorn and Eris in Aries occurred 7 times. In 2020-21, this event occurs with 5 passes.

There is the only a single instance of this particular event, the **last quarter square from Capricorn to Aries**, previously occurring in recorded history. It happened in 691 BCE, in the middle of the Axial Age. At this time, five major thought streams emerged, springing from five great thinkers in different parts of the world:

Buddha in India

Zoroaster in Persia

Confucius in China

Pythagoras in Greece

Hesiod writes Theogony

The Chinese invent printing

The sacred Hindu texts the Upanishads were written.

Mesopotamian power transferred from Assyria to Babylon with the fall of Nineveh

In the past, the long term consequences of these squares to Eris generated global dramatic changes, leaps in new technology for the age, and new awareness and consciousness with each visitation. As a species that learns through emotional experience, we grow through crisis. This correlates the the archetype of Virgo. The Virgo process prepares us to be in society, to live together as equals, peacefully, grounded in natural law.

This is what all of the mystics, religious teachers, wiseman, shamans, and visionaries have told us through the ages. The messages are in the field again.

Individual Chart Analyses

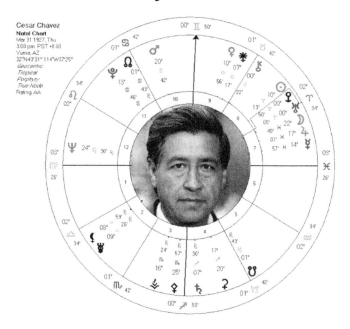

Cesar Chavez
Natal Chart
Mar 31 1927, Thu
3:00 pm PST +8:00
Yuma, AZ
32°N43'31" 114°W37'25"
Geocentric
Tropical
Porphyry
True Node
Rating AA

Cesar Chavez was an American farm worker, labor leader and civil rights activist, who co-founded the United Farm Workers. His deep-seated passion and vision, and the dynamic role he played in the Hispanic community, correlates to his 11th House Pluto in Cancer, ruled by his 7th House Pisces Moon which is conjunct Uranus-Eris at 0° Aries. Uranus and Eris also form a Stellium with his Aries Sun.

Cesar Chavez's motto was *"Si, se puede"* (Spanish for, "Yes, it is possible") conveying his courageous, non-violent stance.

His 10th House Mars in Gemini forms a waning Last Quarter square to his Pisces Moon and forms a partile Gibbous Opposition to his 4th House Ceres in Sagittarius. His initiative and his love of the land drove him to air his grassroots message for worker equality, until it surfaced in the national media. Even-

97

tually Cesar Chavez became an icon and role model for labor organizers across the country.

Back Ground Texture by Ragdollou812
Pic from Google

Fidel Castro is a Marxist-Leninist Cuban political leader. He helped lead the Cuban Revolution and was the President of Cuba from 1978 to 2008. He allied with the Soviet Union during the Cold War, precipitating the Cuban Missile Crisis. Under his authority, Cuba became the first Communist state in the Western Hemisphere.

Through his active support of leftist regimes he earned a place of leadership and respect in the Third World community. He is regarded as a champion of socialism, anti-imperialism, and humanitarianism.

This revolutionary attitude is reflected by Castro's 1st House Pluto in Cancer in a Full Phase Quincunx to its in 8th House Moon in Aquarius ruler. The Moon opposes his 2nd House Leo

Sun conjunct 3rd House Neptune in Leo. 10th House Uranus and Eris in Aries closely straddle Jupiter. Pluto also forms a partile Sesquiquadrate to 6th House Saturn in Sagittarius. He said,

> "Quality of life lies in knowledge, in culture, values are what constitute true quality of life, the supreme quality of life, even above food, shelter and clothing."

There was an instinctive alienation from culture into which he was born which led him to challenge what he perceived to be a limiting political structure and to establish a new future for Cuba.

He said,

> "A revolution is a fight to the death between the future and the past. Condemn me, It does not matter, history will absolve me.""

There was a compelling need to actualize the patriotic vision that he held onto so fiercely. He moved comfortably into his leadership role, after the revolution achieving recognition and support on the world stage.

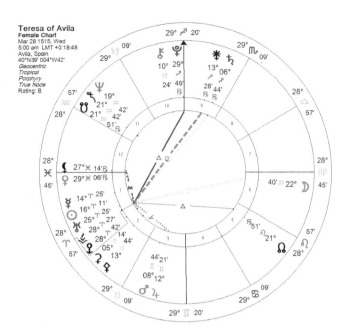

Teresa of Avila
Female Chart
Mar 28 1515, Wed
5:00 am LMT +0:18:48
Avila, Spain
40°N39' 004°W42'
Geocentric
Tropical
Porphyry
True Node
Rating: B

Teresa of Avila

Teresa of Avila was a Spanish noblewoman who felt called to convent life in the Catholic Church. Eris conjunct Vesta (partile) to Uranus trining Pluto, with Mercury, Sun, Uranus, Vesta, and Eris in Aries in her 1st House and Mars conjunct Jupiter in Gemini 3rd House accurately reflects her life as a Carmelite nun, prominent Spanish mystic, religious reformer, author, theologian of the contemplative life and of mental prayer. Active during the Catholic Reformation, she reformed the Carmelite Orders of both women and men.

Teresa was dogged by early family losses and ill health. In her mature years, she became the central figure of a movement of spiritual and monastic renewal borne out of an inner conviction and honed by ascetic practice.

She was also at the center of deep ecclesiastical controversy as she took on the pervasive laxity in her order against the background of the Protestant reformation sweeping over Europe and the Spanish Inquisition asserting church discipline in her home country.

The consequences were to last well beyond her life. She was described as a "restless wanderer, disobedient, and stubborn femina who, under the title of devotion, invented bad doctrines, moving outside the cloister against the rules of the Council of Trent and her prelates; teaching as a master against Saint Paul's orders that women should not teach.

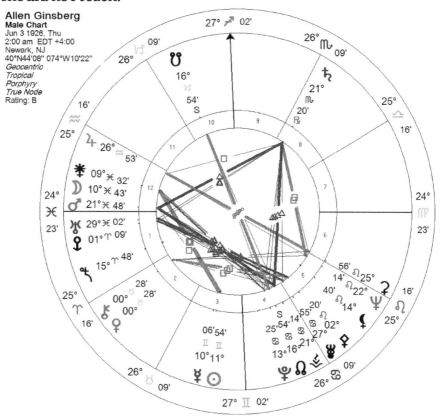

Allen Ginsberg
Male Chart
Jun 3 1926, Thu
2:00 am EDT +4:00
Newark, NJ
40°N44'08" 074°W10'22"
Geocentric
Tropical
Porphyry
True Node
Rating: B

Allen Ginsberg

Born with Eris in Aries conjunct Mars 12th House-Uranus Pisces 1st House, Pisces rising well describes Irwin Allen Ginsberg as an American poet and writer.

As a student at Columbia University in the 1940s, he began friendships with William S. Burroughs and Jack Kerouac, forming the core of the Beat Generation. He vigorously opposed militarism, economic materialism, and sexual repression, and he embodied various aspects of this counterculture with his views on drugs, hostility to bureaucracy, and openness to Eastern religions.

Ginsberg is best known for his poem "Howl" in which he denounced what he saw as the destructive forces of cap

italism and conformity in the United States. San Francisco police and US Customs seized "Howl" in 1956, and it attracted widespread publicity in 1957 when it became the subject of an obscenity trial, as it described heterosexual and homosexual sex at a time when sodomy laws made homosexual acts a crime in every state.

The poem reflected Ginsberg's own sexuality and his relationships with a number of men, including Peter Orlovsky, his lifelong partner. Judge Clayton W. Horn ruled that "Howl" was not obscene: "Would there be any freedom of press or speech if one must reduce his vocabulary to vapid innocuous euphemisms?

Ginsberg was a Buddhist who studied Eastern religious disciplines extensively. He lived modestly, buying his clothing in second-hand stores and residing in apartments in New York's East Village. One of his most influential teachers was Tibetan Buddhist Chagyam Trungpa, the founder of the Naropa Institute in Boulder, Colorado.

Ginsberg took part in decades of political protest against everything from the Vietnam War to the War on Drugs. His collection The Fall of America shared the annual National Book Award for Poetry in 1974. In 1979, he received the National Arts Club gold medal and was inducted into the American Academy of Arts and Letters. He was a Pulitzer Prize finalist in 1995 for his book Cosmopolitan Greetings: Poems 1986 1992.

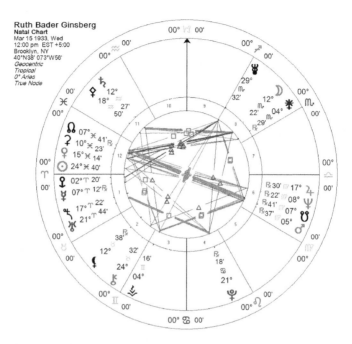

Ruth Bader Ginsberg

Ruth Bader Ginsburg has Eris conjunct Mercury in Aries Rx. Mars conjoins the lunar south node, Neptune, and Jupiter in Virgo all Rx

She is an American lawyer and jurist who is an Associate Justice of the U.S. Supreme Court. She is the second female justice (after Sandra Day O'Connor) of four to be confirmed to the court (along with Sonia Sotomayor and Elena Kagan, who are still serving). Following O'Connor's retirement, and until Sotomayor joined the court, Ginsburg was the only female justice on the Supreme Court.

During that time, Ginsburg became more forceful with her dissents, which were noted by legal observers and in popular culture. She is generally viewed as belonging to the liberal wing of the court.

Ginsburg was born in Brooklyn, New York. Her older sister died when she was a baby, and her mother, one of her biggest sources of encouragement, died shortly before Ginsburg graduated from high school. She then earned her bachelor's degree at Cornell University, and became a wife and mother before starting law school at Harvard, where she was one of the few women in her class. Ginsburg transferred to Columbia Law School, where she graduated tied for first in her class. Following law school, Ginsburg turned to academia. She was a professor at Rutgers Law School and Columbia Law School, teaching civil procedure as one of the few women in her field.

Ginsburg spent a considerable part of her legal career as an advocate for the advancement of gender equality and women's rights, winning multiple victories arguing before the Supreme Court. Ginsburg has received attention in American popular culture for her fiery liberal dissents and refusal to step down; she has been dubbed "The Notorious R.B.G."

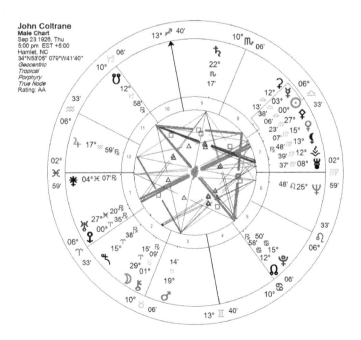

John Coltrane

John Coltrane was an American jazz saxophonist and composer. Working in the bebop and hard bop idioms early in his career, Coltrane was at the forefront of free jazz. He led at least fifty recording sessions and appeared on many albums by other musicians, including trumpeter Miles Davis and pianist Thelonious Monk.

John Coltrane had Eris conjunct Uranus in Pisces in his 1st House. Eris opposes Sun, Mercury in Libra, Pallas Athene in Virgo in his 7th House. His Mars in Taurus 3rd trins Venus in Virgo.

Over the course of his career, Coltrane's music took on an increasingly spiritual dimension. He remains one of the most influential saxophonists in music history. He received many posthumous awards, including canonization by the African Orthodox Church and a Pulitzer Prize in 2007.

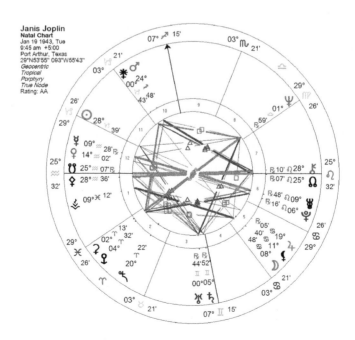

Janis Joplin

"She goes barefooted when she feels like it, wears Levis to class because they're more comfortable, and carries her autoharp with her everywhere she goes so that in case she gets the urge to break into song, it will be handy. Her name is Janis Joplin. "

https://www.washingtonpost.com/wp-srv/style/features/joplin.htm

Janis Joplin was born in Port Arthur, Texas, on January 19, 1943, to Dorothy Bonita East, a registrar at a business college, and her husband, Seth Ward Joplin, an engineer at Texaco. She had two younger siblings, Michael and Laura. The family belonged to the Churches of Christ denomination.

As a teenager, Joplin befriended a group of outcasts, one of whom had albums by blues artists Bessie Smith, Ma Rainey, and Lead Belly, whom Joplin later credited with influencing her decision to become a singer. She began singing blues and folk music with friends at Thomas Jefferson High School.

Joplin stated that she was ostracized and bullied in high school. As a teen, she became overweight and suffered from acne, leaving her with deep scars that required dermabrasion. Other kids at high school would routinely taunt her and call her names like "pig," "freak," "nigger lover," or "creep."

She stated,

"I was a misfit. I read, I painted, I thought. I didn't hate niggers."

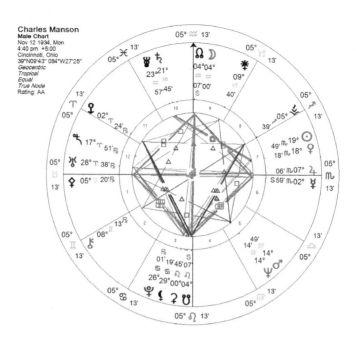

Charles Manson

Born to a 16-year-old mother, never knew his father
Mother and stepfather sentenced to prison term for grand larceny. When he was 9 years old he set his school on fire. At age 13 he was placed in a strict school for delinquent boys run by the Catholic Church. Committed his first crime at age 18. He was sent to 2 different reform schools. He was schooled in crime by a friend's father who was a professional thief. He was gang raped and beaten in school and ran away 18 times. He was imprisoned twice.

In early August 1969, Manson encouraged his followers to start a race war by committing murders in the Los Angeles area, and making the killings appear to be racially motivated.

His savior complex reflects his Eris in Aries in his 12th House, ruled by Mars partile conjunct to Neptune in Virgo, 5th House. Eris trines Pluto, conjoins Lilith in Cancer, Ceres, and the Lunar South Node in Leo in his 4th House, resulting in his radical compulsion for antisocial behavior.

A Grand cross across the axes of the chart: Moon-Lunar nodes-Uranus, Pallas, ASC, Pluto, Ceres, Lilith, Mercury, Jupiter, relative to Pluto in Cancer ruled by Moon Aquarius 10 House, conjunct the lunar north node. Uranus in Aries, 12th House, conjoins Pallas Athene and Ascendant in Gemini. Jupiter in his 7th House conjoins Mercury station direct, in his 6th House in Scorpio. Moon conjoin his Lunar North Node stationed direct in his 9th House.

Clearly this is someone with a most disruptive personality that thrived on chaos.

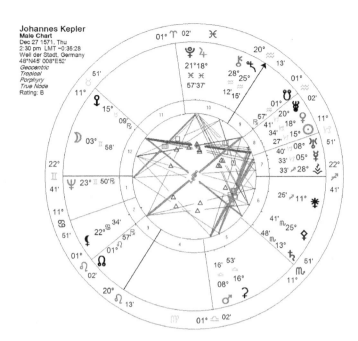

Johannes Kepler

Key figure in the 17th-century scientific revolution, known for his laws of planetary motion. Kepler's laws of planetary motion, three scientific laws describing the motion of planets around the Sun, published by Johannes Kepler between 1609 and 1619.

These improved the heliocentric theory of Nicolaus Copernicus, replacing its circular orbits with elliptical trajectories, and explaining how planetary velocities vary.

His work provided one of the foundations for Newton's theory of universal gravitation. Kepler was a student of Tycho Brahe -- an astronomer, astrologer, and alchemist. His mother was a healer and herbalist.

Kepler was introduced to astronomy at an early age. At age six, he observed the Great Comet of 1577, writing that,

> "he was taken by his mother to a high place to look at it."

He studied philosophy, mathematics, and astronomy ~ Learned

both the Ptolemaic and Copernican systems of planetary motion. Kepler Defended the heliocentric view.

His Eris in Taurus Rx in his12th House made him a practical visionary, looking for universal truth. Eris's focus equals our essential work. With Venus conjunct Sun, 8th House (dispositer of Eris), and Uranus, Mercury [chart ruler] 7th House all in Capricorn, and Pluto in Pisces conjunct Jupiter in 10th House he was absolutely compeled to search for truth. Neptune conjunct his Gemini ascendant in 1st House (opposite Vesta Sagittarius 7th) kicked it up a notch to the Search for Ultimate Truth.

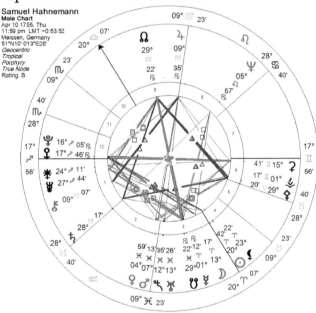

Samuel Hahnemann
Male Chart
Apr 10 1755, Thu
11:59 pm LMT −0:53:52
Meissen, Germany
51°N10' 013°E28'
Geocentric
Tropical
Porphyry
True Node
Rating: B

Samuel Hahnemann

Hahnemann was dissatisfied with the state of medicine in his time,~particularly such as bloodletting...medicine that did the patient more harm than good:

> "My sense of duty would not easily allow me to treat the unknown pathological state of my suffering brethren with these unknown medicines. The thought of becoming in this way a murderer or malefactor towards the life of my fellow human beings was most terrible to me, so terrible and disturbing that I wholly

> gave up my practice in the first years of my married life and oc-
> cupied myself solely with chemistry and writing."

After giving up his practice around 1784, Hahnemann resolved to investigate the causes of medicine's alleged errors.

While translating "A Treatise on the Materia Medica", Hahnemann encountered the claim that cinchona, the bark of a Peruvian tree, was effective in treating malaria because of its astringency.

Noting that the drug induced malaria-like symptoms in himself, he concluded that it would do so in any healthy individual.

Eris conjunct Pluto in Sagittarius 12th House conjunct Ascendant, opposing Ceres in Gemini 6th House correlates to his compelling need to actualize the truth of his inner understanding and ground his ideas in practical work regarding healthcare.

His Jupiter Rx in Virgo 9 House, partile trine to Chiron Capricorn in 1st House, opposite Venus, Mars, in Pisces in 2nd House, Uranus Pisces 3rd House generated life choices made according to deeply committed (Juno Sagittarius 1st House) to his essential values and priorities.

Mars ruled by the Dark of the Moon in Aries ~ greatly intensified his inner compulsion to embody his beliefs, intellectual understanding, into his life's work with medicine. This led him to postulate a healing principle:

> "that which can produce a set of symptoms in a healthy individual, can treat a sick individual who is manifesting a similar set of symptoms."

This principle, like cures like, became the basis for an approach to medicine which he gave the name homeopathy.

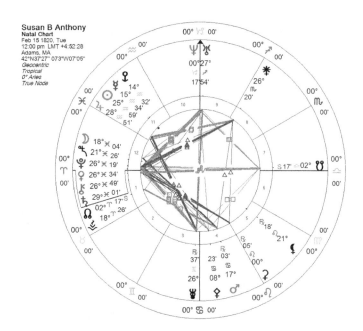

Susan B Anthony

Social reformer and women's rights activist, Anthony held a pivotal role in women's suffrage movement

Her Eris conjunct Mercury Aquarius 9th House (chart ruler) made her an outspoken public speaker.

Uranus in Sagittarius conjoins Neptune Capricorn, 7th House resulting in her vision of how society should function.

Pluto in Pisces, 10th House conjunct Moon, Venus, Saturn, Chiron, and Sedna (and Saturn).

Susan Anthonty was born a Quaker, in a family that shared apassion for social reform, supported anti-slavery

Her father was an abolitionist and temperance advocate.

Mars in Cancer Rx in 2nd House gave her values concerning family and gender issues. Eris in Aquarius 11th House, Bi-quintile Pallas Athene Cancer 4th House

delivered an emotional embodiment of higher messages, meetung the world as spiritual warrior.

112

All of these individuals, in their own way, have shown a radical expression of their personality, or the need to overcome extreme misfortune.

Individuals with Eris in the 1st House:
John Coltrane
Nostradamus

Individuals with Eris in the 2nd House:
Thomas Edison
Adolf Eichmann
Truman Capote
Jane Fonda
J Edgar Hoover

Individuals with Eris in the 3rd House:
Michaelangelo
Sandra Day O €™Conner
Angelica HustonCharles Dickens
Dane Rudhyar
L Ron Hubbard
Malcolm X

Individuals with Eris in the 4th House:
Leonardo
Mozart
Louis Pasteur
Charles Manson

Individuals with Eris in the 5th House:
Ghandi
Adolf Hitler
Jackie Onassis
Thomas More
Margaret Thatcher s
George Harrison
Vladimir Putin

Grace Kelly

Individuals with Eris in the 6th House:
John Kennedy
Churchill
Walt Disney
Rudolph Valentino

Individuals with Eris in the 7th House:
Henry Ford
Orville Wright
Caesar Chavez
Hugh Hefner
Paul Simon
Dolly Parton

Individuals with Eris in the 8th House:
Issac Newton
Frida Kahlo
Marilyn Monroe
Mohammed Ali
Maya Angelou
Andy Warhol
Donald Trump
Elton John

Individuals with Eris in the 9th House:
Joan of Arc
Anne Frank
Vincent Van Gogh

Individuals with Eris in the 10th House:
Orson Welles
Judy Garland
Fidel Castro
Albert Einstein
Miles Davis

Individuals with Eris in the 11th House:
Martin Luther King
Johannes Kepler
Abraham Lincoln
Samuel Hahnemann
Alexander Graham Bell
Amelia Earhart
Charles Manson

Individuals with Eris in the 12th House:
John Lennon
Johannes Kepler
Samuel Hahnemann
Abraham Lincoln
Margaret Sanger
Joseph McCarthy

Conclusions

The themes from the past offer us a glimpse of the future. The world has shrunk and the world has exploded. Somehow, the world did not become a safe for democracy, or even seem to be safe at all. Recent history is as compelling as it is disturbing.

The food that we eat, the water that we drink, and the air that we breathe, all are under attack by acts of commission and omission.

Xenophobia, racism, mysogeny, endless war, economic disparity, lawlessness, the rise of authoriatarianism, famine, terrorism, religious persecution, and political corruption are rampant around the world. As if that was not enough we are under the health and social exigencies of COVID-19.

On the whole, the world population is only now beginning to recognize of the enormity of the ways our lives have been altered in order to make it more cororately profitable.

The result is the deterioration of the quality of the American diet and the overwhelming incidence of cancer, heart disease, and diabetes, mostly among Blacks, Hispanics, Asians, and Native Americans. At the same time, the cost of healthcare has risen, on the average, 5-7% annually, placing it out of the reach of those who need it the most. COVID has already shown that the most vulnerable segments of the population are non-white.

Government regulatory agencies, mandated to safeguard natural resources have become "privatized". The oligarchs now make up their own rules and regulations, using whatever means available to cheaply and efficiently extract natural resources, wherever they can find them. There is a revolving door between Wall Street and Washington, as Federal officials and corporate officers regularly exchange roles. There is no legistlative oversight, and the rule of law is under seige. In essence, the United States faces it greatest test of the rule of law in its 400 years of history.

The financial markets are supported by make-believe money and financial instruments constructed from worthless equities.

In the United States the incidence of gun violence has escalated to a level unprecedented in history. Law enforcement is has become the refuge for PTSD stricken ex-military with the collateral damage being inflicted mostly on people of color, or ethnic diversity.

Beyond our borders, US Military forces are being challenged by BRIC nations in both hemispheres. Foreign state agents compromise high-level US corporate and government networks with alacrity, helping themselves to classified military and sensitive financial and medical records with alarming ease. Even worse, the US policy of interfering with elections in other countries has come home to roost as Russian, Chinese, and Iranian assets regularly troll social media planting fake news.

Large numbers of American voters have become disenfranchised either because they feel politically and economically disempowered, or simply through disinterest. Financial markets are again experiencing record highs, punctuated by erratic, and potentially critical downside events, paralleling the runup to the 1929 Crash.

The totality of the amount of assets in play is able to keep the ball in the air, but to many observers it is clearly a fiduciary juggling act.

It is not my intention to add to the litany of fear mongering that has proliferated the media. There is a law of saturation that predicates the idea that change does not occur until the desire that is generating the same wrong choice, over and over again, finally reaches its saturation point, and must precipitate out, and make a different more conscious choice. It is human nature to maintain self-consistency. What is familiar is safe. We hold onto what we know, because what is unknown is scary. When the pain becomes greater than the fear, we change.

Perhaps the circumstantial and political crises are the homeopathic remedy needed to heal the emotional toxins that have resided in the collective shadow for centuries and perhaps millenia. History fails to remind us that xenophobia and religious intolerance came over on the Mayflower.

Astrology and Hindu philosophy describe extremely long cycles of evolution. Swami Sri Yukteswar, astrologer, and teacher of Paramahansa Yogananda, elaborately described the cycle of the the Yugas, a 24,000-year cycle that correlates to, and historically illuminates the precession of the equinoxes.

There is evidence on our planet of civilizations that flourished in a Golden Age, long before recorded history. The Great Pyramid, Stonehenge, Gobekli Tepe, Chichen Itza, Tikal, Chaco Canyon, are all evidence of unexplained advanced technologies. If we stretch out the timeframe of the Earth on the scale of a single 24-hour day, we are only aware of the last few minutes of its history.

In recent years the work of Erich von Daniken, Mike Brenner, the late Marshall Klarfeld, and other researchers have produced hard evidence that what we call the "stone age" was not primitive at all. 5,000 years from now, what evidence will remain of our contemporary culture? Certainly not anything made of paper, cloth, wood, glass, plastic, or perhaps even steel.

The Uranus Eris conjunctions of 2015-16, under a Mutable Cross, reflect an open channel for radical new imaginings and new ideas to spontaneously emerge, and the practical ways of integrating and self-actualizing these new paradigms. The intention is to build a new framework and allow new visions to re-dream and re-imagine ourselves and the world. The current

Pluto-Saturn conjunctions shows us the current limits of our beliefs and visions.

As the Lunar Nodes move through truth-oriented Gemini and Sagittarius, all truths will come under close scrutiny. What we believed to be gospel will be exposed as heresy. What was considered heresy will be illuminated as truth. What we are searching for is not just truth, but Ultimate Truth. Jupiter opens up our understanding, and create the space for new perspectives, and Neptune whispers knowledge from the Ancestors.

Have we reached the saturation point where the scales begin to shift? From a certain perspective, the events of our lives, individually and collectively unfold with exquisite perfection, and meaning. Each episode, each consequence, is flawless and seamless, arriving at exactly the right time, with exactly the right intensity. What the ancient Greeks called "kairos".

The Law of Correspondences states, "As above, so below, as below, so above." The Universe is interactive. Our outer world is simply the mirror of our inner world. Let us all rest assured that we have not been too overly optimistic in our pre-life planning.

References

Since Babylonian times, prior to 1781 and the discovery of Uranus, Saturn was considered to be the outermost planet in the solar system. The discovery of Uranus was astronomically revolutionary. Not only did it also have rings like Saturn, but it also spins on its side, at a 90 ° angle to the ecliptic. New celestial bodies are discovered, come into our awareness, as the development of human consciousness unfolds

http://www.sacred-texts.com/cla/hesiod/works.htm">http://www.sacred-texts.com/cla/hesiod/works.htm

http://www.vlib.us/medieval/lectures/
national_monarchies.html

https://en.wikipedia.org/wiki/Population_history_of_indi-
genous_peoples_of_the_Americas €

https://en.wikipedia.org/wiki/Fidel_Castro

https://en.wikipedia.org/wiki/Individuation

http://www.perseus.tufts.edu/hopper/text?doc=Perseus
%3Atext%3A1999.03.0011%3Aact=5%3Ascene=

http://www.sacred-texts.com/cla/homer/ili/index.htm

THE TRUE CHART OF
THE UNITED STATES

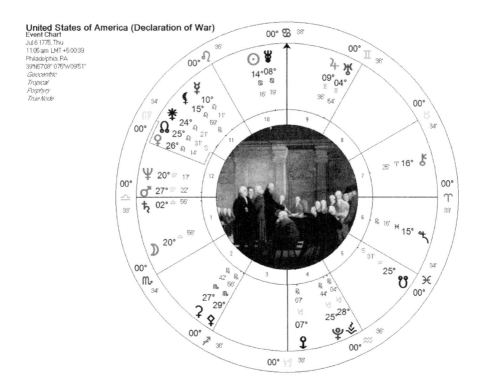

United States of America (Declaration of War)
Event Chart
Jul 6 1775, Thu
11:06 am LMT +5:00:39
Philadelphia, PA
39°N57'08" 075°W09'51"
Geocentric
Tropical
Porphyry
True Node

Late in the morning of July 6, 1775, the 2nd Continental Congress passed acts "to bear arms" against Great Britain, and to establish a standing army. The next day they named George Washington as Commander in Chief. Those legislative acts by default severed all economic and political connections to our mother country.

Prior to this date, the naval embargo and the skirmishes with the British Redcoats at Lexington and Concord had been defensive actions. On July 6th, 1775, the Colonies assumed an offensive military stance. As of this date in history, the 13 American Colonies were no longer colonies of Great Britain. They became a sovereign independent state.

I came to this chart by way of my friend Arielle Guttman, who collaborated for a time with the late Jim Lewis, realizer of Astro*Cartography. Jim believed that this chart was the true chart of the United States. I have been working with this chart for the last year of so, with some surprisingly accurate results. Especially the current events unfolding as this is being written in 2020. I would point readers to my YouTube, "America At The Crossroads". There are 51 partile (exact, same degree) aspects to the Declaration of War chart and election day, November 3rd, 2020. https://youtu.be/oezZOZ9i1sM

American Cultural Diversity

The United States was founded by settlers who were primarily from Europe. They came from a variety of countries bringing with them not only different cultural heritages and customs, but also different worldviews, religions, and philosophies.

There was Dutch and Spanish tradition, as well as French, Italian, Portuguese, and African. Neither were they were all Christian. In 1492, the Jews were expelled from Spain. Columbus' ships sailed from Spain.

US National Conditioning

The analysis of any chart from an Evolutionary Astrology perspectivice must begin by understanding the context of the charas, the conditioning that was brought forward. In other words, "what has come before". This information is contained in Pluto, by its sign and house, and by the aspects it makes to other planets and asteroids in the chart.

It is most important to understand the conditioning of the person or entity. In this case, the national conditioning consists of the various throught streams and belief systems of the original settlers, and founders. The United States was founded by settlers who were primarily from Europe. They came from different countries bringing with them not only different cultural heritages and customs, but also different worldviews.

Most were driven from their respective homelands seeking freedom of expression, fleeing the severe suppression and repression their spiritual beliefs. What has happened over many centuries is that those who sought the exercise of freedom, became the new suppressors.

It is important to remember that for the first 170 years, the 13 American Colonies were British, living according to English law and tradition. It was pointed out to me by my friend, Michael Pulman, retired Professor of History at the University of Colorado, that the causes of the American Civil War stem from the English Civil War, 200 years earlier between the Parlamentarians and the Royalists. For the most part the Royalists were awarded land grants south of what is now the Mason Dixon Line, and settled the Southern Colonies. The Parlamentarians for the most part, along with Dutch and German Protestants established the Northern Colonies.
These unresolved issues and viewpoints of governance, and human rights seeded the thoughtstreams of the colonies.

Puritanism

History highlights the landing of the Pilgrim on Plymouth Rock, in what is now the State of Massachusetts. Consensu holds the belief that the Puritans arrived to establish a foothold on personal freedoms. Unfortunately, the opposite is true. The origins of US national xenophobia also arrived o the Mayflower. Because the native they encountered were living simply in a what was seen as a primitive state with housing built from natural materials, the settlers viewed the indigenous people they encountered as "savages".

The spiritual beliefs their brought were also narrow. Puritanism taught the singular righteousness and sovereignty of God. God directed all things by exercise of his will. The Puritan belief structure provided for God choosing those who were deemed worthy for salvation. All human beings were pledged by a strict covenant and code of behavior, and were severely condemned for failure to adhere to it. The threat of fire and brimstone would be realized. Human beings, especially women, were portrayed as depraved sinners, and women were often portrayed as witches and burned at the stake.

The Family

This thought stream is still active in the United States. The best example of is the most influential, yet unknown organization known as "The Family". The Family is a U.S.-based religious and political organization. The Fellowship holds one regular public event each year, the National Prayer Breakfast, which is held in Washington, D.C. in February each year. Every sitting United States president since Dwight D. Eisenhower has participated in at least one National Prayer Breakfast during his term. This event has taken place every year since 1953. It is attended by ~3500 guests, including international invitees from over 100 countries.

The group's known participants include ranking United States government officials, corporate executives, heads of religious and humanitarian aid organizations, and ambassadors and high-ranking politicians from across the world. Many United States senators and congressmen have publicly acknowledged working with the Fellowship or are documented as having worked together to pass or influence legislation. NETFLIX-THE FAMILY https://www.netflix.com/title/80063867 The influence of what has become known as the "religious right" is a pervasive, "top down" directive that seeks to control the political direction of the United States; a country that was founded on the principle of separation of Church and state.

The Conquistadors ("Conquerors")

The Conquistadors were knights, explorers of Spain and Portugal, professional soldiers of fortune, seeking to expand the influence of Spain the new New World, looking for gold in indigenous cultures. They used European tactics; firearms, and cavalry against less sophisticated spears and bows and arrows. Their victories were facilitated by old world European diseases, smallpox, flu, and typhus, for which the indigenous tribes had no acquired immunity.

Entire tribes of the New World were decimated as a result of disease. One famous story is of an native called Tisquantum, known as "Squanto". Some believe that Tisquantum was captured as a young man on what is now the coast of Maine in 1605. Tisquantum was captured and brought to England. He eventually returned to America in 1619 working as an interpreter. Tisquantum searched for his homeland but tragically, he arrived as the "Great Dying" reached its horrific climax. His tribe had all been wiped out. His home village, Patuxet, was lost. He was the only surviving member of his tribe.

Also ccompanying the soldiers were religious missionaries, converting the "savage" indigenous tribes to European ways of thinking. Non-military occupants also sailed on the Spanish galleons; French and Italians, and Jews seeking refuge from the Spanish Inquisition, who along with the soldiers and missionaries, would become the oldest inhabited settlements, and family lineages in the United States.

Freemasonry

In addition to the religious conditioning brought with the early settlers, Gnosticism was also practiced. Gnosis is defined as the knowledge of transcendence arrived at by way of interior, intuitive means, rather than through human intermediaries of priests and self-appointed religious leaders. The personal direct experience of God, the Source-of-All-That-Is was their intention, through intuition, dreams, and inner practices. Freemasonry expresses itself through the medium of symbolism and myth. The Masons built many of the important National buildings & monuments, incorporating in them traditional occult and astrological symbolism.

Some of the more notable founding fathers to also be masons including George Washington, Ben Franklin leader of the Pennsylvania chapter, Paul Revere leader of the Massachusetts chapter, John Hancock , and Chief Justice John Marshall who greatly influenced the shaping of the Supreme Court.

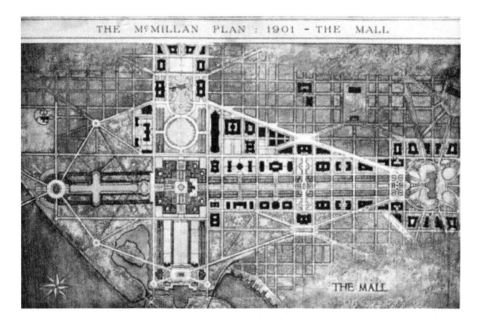

All together it is believed that about nine of the fifty-six men that signed the Declaration of Independence were masons, and about thirteen of the thirty-nine that signed the US Constitutions were also masons.

By the time of the American Revolution slavery had been institutionalized. Many of the Founding Fathers were slave owners. Slavery was the single most important component of the agrarian economy of the Southern Colonies. Slavery however was not limited to the South. The invention of the cotton gin only increased the economic dependency on the practice of slavery. The role of slavery beca,e the most contentious issue during the drafting of the U.S. Constitution. It was also the incendiary issue that ignited the American Civil War.

US Pluto Capricorn 4ᵗʰ House

Ruler of the 2ⁿᵈ House:
THE ECONOMY,
STOCK MARKET, BANKS
Mundane Astrology:
NUCLEAR POWER,
TERRORISM,THE MAFIA

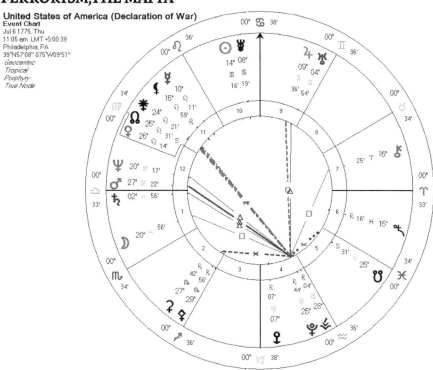

United States of America (Declaration of War)
Event Chart
Jul 6 1775, Thu
11:05 am LMT +5:00:39
Philadelphia, PA
39°N57'08" 075°W09'51"
Geocentric
Tropical
Porphyry
True Node

The first American settlers were exiles from their homeland. They left their homeland in order to be able to practice their beliefs. (Lunar South Node Aquarius 6th House)

They were religious refugees fleeing persecution, and soldiers of fortune seeking treasure and royal recognition. (Pluto Capricorn 4th House applies to a disseminating trine to Mars-Neptune 12th House)

They had lost their own homeland so they had no reluctance to usurp the homeland of the indigenous people of the land they "discovered". They transferred their wounding experience onto the "primitive" people they encountered.
(Pluto Capricorn 4; Chiron Aries 7th House applies to a crescent square to Pluto Capricorn 4th)

They were driven by idealism to create a new future, a destiny insured by divine intention. (Pluto Capricorn 4th partile full phase quincunx to the Lunar North Node Aquarius 11, Uranus conjunct Jupiter Gemini 9th)

The New World became their surrogate homeland. They brought with them memories of past trauma, persecution, and oppression. (Ceres Scorpio 2nd applies to a last quarter sextile to Pluto Capricorn 4th House)

They came to meet the New World with their self-empowerment as the reigning authority. (Pluto Capricorn 4 trine Saturn Libra 1st)

Their sense of God-given self-importance and intellectual conceit empowered them to exert their sense of superiority without moral compass. (Jupiter Gemini 9th separates from a 1st quarter sesquisquare to Pluto Capricorn 4th; Uranus Gemini 9th separates from a 1st quarter trine to Pluto)

Their sense of self importance allowed for ethnic inequality and generated a distorted sense of self-worth. (Moon Libra 1 applies to a last quarter square Pluto Capricorn 4th).

This all important Pluto placement correlates to US Homeland, and a past history of the loss of homeland. The original European settlers were exiles, immigrants, and refugees from their mother country. For one reason or another they were forced to leave, some under threat of imprisonment or death. This karmic memory of native displacement was transferred onto the indigenous people encountered in the newly discovered territories of North and South America; native peoples whom they called "savages" reflecting an inherent disregard for indigenous history, culture, spiritual practices, or lifestyle.

The underlying themes also were about security, safety, and survival. From the very beginning, the early settlements were faced with challenges to their very survival by the simple demands of food and shelter. The Roanoke settlement failed. The Plymouth settlement also nearly collapsed. The earliest settlement in Santa Fe, and the later settlement in St. Augustine by the Spanish took root, built upon deep Catholic traditions.

Their beliefs, as well as the Protestant beliefs in the north fostered strong patriarchal family values. Because the sense of place, the importance of the homeland holds such power, Nationalism, the belief that adopts a vertical posture of national importance, holds sway in the national shadow. The Capricorn archetype needs to assume and assert authority. The retrograde condition of Pluto deepens the sense of loss; "We lost our home so we will just take yours."

The close proximity of Vesta (separating from a new phase conjunction) generates crises in the development of national authenticity. The need is to learn commitment to self authenticity. Just as individuals must cope with the spread between intention and action, so do national entities. As we will observe when we analyze the US lunar nodes, the evolutionary trajectory points towards self-enlightened idealism.
Unfortunately US history, as it unfolded expressed more splintered, self-interest than focus on what was best for the collective as a whole.

Challenges from Venus in Leo (separating from a full phase inconjunct) can exhibit both the magnetic and shadow traits of Aphrodite; her vanity, her need for adoration, and her venge-fullness when she is thwarted.

There is a militarized readiness to meet the world as its police forece (Mars Virgo | Saturn Libra rising) and to fight to maintain control using direct forceful intervention when deemed neces-sary, (Mars Virgo 12th House), using hidden agendas, and clan-destine methods when necessary (Neptune Virgo 12th House).

The Pluto archetype and the Capricorn archetype both have control issues, they need to be the authority. The power struc-ture is built on uniquely individual, yet personal truths.
There is a facility to wound others without conscience or re-morse driven by memories of past trauma, persecution, and op-pression.

US Lunar Nodes

North Node Leo 11th House
South Node Aquarius 5th House

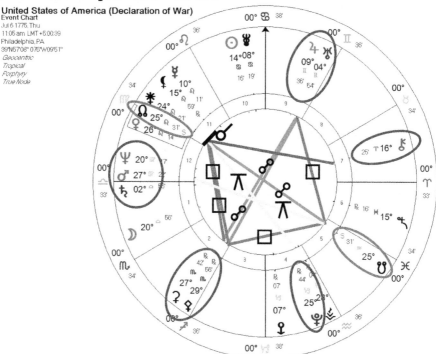

United States of America (Declaration of War)
Event Chart
Jul 6 1775, Thu
11:05 am LMT +5:00:39
Philadelphia, PA
39°N57'08" 075°W09'51"
Geocentric
Tropical
Porphyry
True Node

The process of synthesizing the needs of the individual and the demands of the collective.

This is the individuation process itself; conscious focus on the process of becoming. How one grows into who they intend to be as part of society. How do we find our own individuality as part of the collective? The original intent of the first settlers was a utopian, and embodied humanitarian perspectives and ideals. Aquarius can seem aloof in their emotional distancing. Discovered at the time of the American and French Revolutions, Uranus correlates to insurrection and rebellion; Independent and inspired, forward thinking. The immigrants and refugees came from a past where personal expression was repressed and individual liberties were denied. Aquarius is exile.

The thread of US History alternates between periods of enlightened advancement, and partisan self interest. (Lunar North Node Leo 11th House separates from a new phase conjunction Venus Leo)

Wanting to assume technological leadership.(Sun 10th)

From the outset political intentions were unconventional, ahead of their time socially and politically, though often expercising proselytizing religious tendencies, and a sense of moral superiority. (Lunar nodes square Jupiter-Uranus Gemini 9th)

Ideological strategies centered on beliefs that the "American Way" is the best way. (Lunar nodes square Jupiter-Uranus Gemini 9th)

Grief from powerless circumstance from the past creates priorities that strategize the desire for control. (Lunar Nodes square Ceres-Pallas Athene Scorpio Rx 2nd House)

A determination to be a world leader politically, militarily, and economically. (North Node new phase conjunction Venus Leo, north node applies to a partile full phase quincunx to Pluto 11, Sun 10th, South Node partile (same degree) quincunx Mars Virgo 12th)

Belief that the US is the world's police force. (Mars Virgo-12th-Saturn Libra 1st-Ascendant; applies to a balsamic conjunction the Ascendant, Mars Virgo 12th separates from a gibbous quincunx lunar south node Aquarius 5th)

"We the People of the United States, in Order to form a more perfect Union, establish Justice, insure domestic Tranquility, provide for the common defence, promote the general Welfare, and secure the Blessings of Liberty to ourselves and our Posterity, do ordain and establish this Constitution for the United States of America."
--Preamble to the United States Constitution September 17, 1787

Planets Square The Nodes "Skipped Steps"

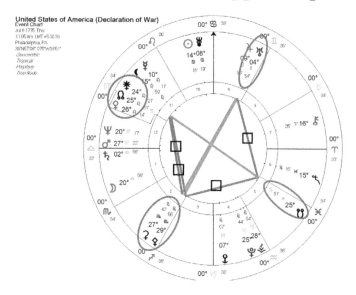

According to Evolutionary Astrology, a planet squaring the lunar nodes describes a condition where a lesson or potential fruition was "skipped over". In our evolutionary progress we don't get to skip any steps in our personal growth along the way. There is no judgement regarding skipped steps. Planet square the lunar nodes indicate that bcause of circumstances, or because the challenge was too difficult, left unfinished, a requirmentto complete the work emerges again as an evolutionary necessity.

The following planets square the US Lunar Nodes.

Uranus Gemini 9th House

This correlates to the need to understand ourselves from a wider perspective. Overcoming the trauma of the past through the pursuit of a more enlightened path forward.

Pallas Athene Scorpio Rx 2nd House

The requirement is to Become self-empowered by embracing a wider vision and worldveiw. There is an ability to see the the wide scope of the entire paradigm, in order to understand how the individual inherent processes within that paradigm are working together. this is about learning to exercise power wisely, not selfishly, rather for the the good of all.

Ceres Scorpio Rx 2nd House

The need to Learn how to share essential resources. Healing the memory of the loss of surviva; being able to self-actualize according one's own natural abilities and inclinations.

US Uranus Gemini 9th House

Ruler of Lunar South Node
Ruler of the 5th House:
CHILDREN,
SOCIAL LIFE, SPORTS

Mundane Astrology
TECHNOLOGY, WILD WEATHER,
DISRUPTIVE EVENTS

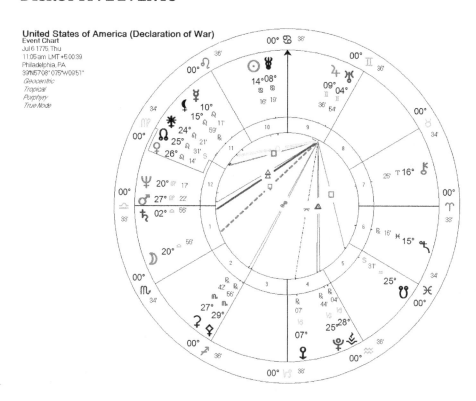

United States of America (Declaration of War)
Event Chart
Jul 6 1775, Thu
11:05 am LMT +5:00:39
Philadelphia, PA
39°N57'08" 075°W09'51"
Geocentric
Tropical
Porphyry
True Node

Trauma experienced from the loss of personal freedoms generates the commitment to the principles of liberty, and equality.
(Moon Libra 1st separating from a gibbous sesquisquare, Venus
applying to a 1st quarter square to Uranus)

The necessity to find embodiment and expression for higher ideals. (Mars Libra 12th applying to a 1st quarter trine, Saturn Libra 1st applying to a 1st quarter trine)

National ideologies and worldview as an amalgam of religious beliefs and gnostic practices. (separating from a new phase conjunction to Jupiter Gemini 9th)

Forward-looking, revolutionary sense of purpose. (Pluto Capricorn Rx 4th separating from a separating from a last quarter trine, Pallas Athene Scorpio Rx separating from a gibbous opposition, applying to a gibbous quincunx to Eris Capricorn Rx 4th)

Memory of past trauma. (Ceres Scorpio Rx separating from a gibbous opposition, Uranus square lunar nodes)

> "We hold these truths to be self-evident, that all Men are created equal, that they are endowed by their Creator with certain unalienable Rights, that among these are Life, Liberty and the Pursuit of Happiness."
>
> IN CONGRESS, JULY 4, 1776

US Sun Cancer 10th House

Ruler of the Lunar North Node
Ruler of the 11th House
Mundane Astrology
CONGRESS
FOREIGN ALLIES

10th House
Mundane Astrology
THE PRESIDENT

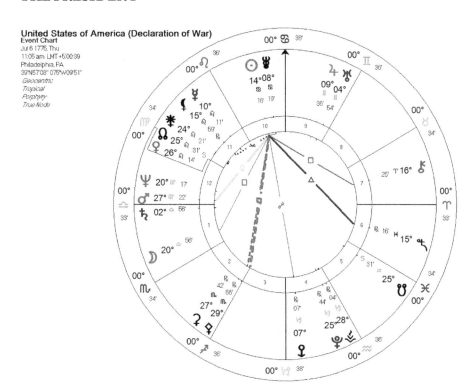

United States of America (Declaration of War)
Event Chart
Jul 6 1776, Thu
11:05 am LMT +5:00:39
Philadelphia, PA
39°N57'08" 075°W09'51"
Geocentric
Tropical
Porphyry
True Node

The United States achieves it status as a world leader (Sun Cancer 10th)

Family values (Sun Cancer 10th)

Safety and security (Sun Cancer 10th)

Prominent role model for self-actuating governance. (Sun Cancer 10th)

Expectation that the President is a "family man", who is the role model of social correctness. (Chiron Aries 7th separating from a last quarter square to Sun Cancer 10th)

National isolationism as well as the need for the President and his adminstration to remain connected and available to the people at large, and to reflect their perspectives. ("Orphaned Sun Cancer)

Crises resulting from an overly patriarchalal governance. (Sun 10th House)

Inner messages... heard or ignored? Enabling the rule of justice and fairness to underlie national directives. (Pallas Athene partile sesquisquare to Sun)

National focus on reputation, occupation, advancement. (On the "Midheaven")

Expectation that the President is a "family man", who is the role model of social correctness (Sun Cancer 10th)

US Moon Libra 1st House

Ruler of the 10th House
THE PRESIDENT

1st House
Mundane Astrology
THE COUNTRY AS A WHOLE
THE PEOPLE AT LARGE
WOMEN

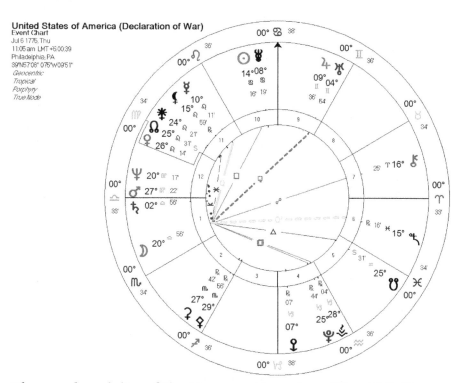

United States of America (Declaration of War)
Event Chart
Jul 6 1775. Thu
11:05 am LMT +5:00:39
Philadelphia; PA
39°N57'08" 075°W09'51"
Geocentric
Tropical
Porphyry
True Node

The synchronicity of the Moon, as the ruler of the 10th House, and resident in the 1st House implies that the President is (was intended to be) a "man of the people". How often the choice of the majority of voters was actually reflected in the outcome of the election is relatively unknown, however recent elections

143

has revealed that there are fallibilities, perhaps flaws, in the design of the US electoral system.

The desire for balance and equality permeates the emotional nature of the people of the United States and the country as a whole. (Moon Libra 1st)

There is a round-robin kind of mutual reception between Venus and the luminaries which blends their archetypes together: The Sun is in the Moon's sign. The Moon is in Venus's sign. Venus is in the Sun's sign. Venusian vanity permeates both the national ego (Moon) and personality (Sun).
Crises persist from the inability to achieve universal racial equality. (Moon Libra 1st separates from a first quarter square to Sun Cancer 10th)

Crises develop when authority is exercised at the expense of the public good. (Moon Libra 1st applies to a last quarter square to Pluto Capricorn 10th)

Wounded history is carried forward in foreign affairs. (Moon Libra 1st applies to a gibbous opposition to Chiron Aries 7th)

US Venus Leo 11th House

Ruler of the 1st
THE COUNTRY
THE PEOPLE AT LARGE
Ruler of the 8th House
PUBLIC MORTALITY
NATIONAL DEBT
SOCIAL SECURITY
Mundane Astrology:
ARTS, ENTERTAINMENT,
WOMEN'S ISSUES

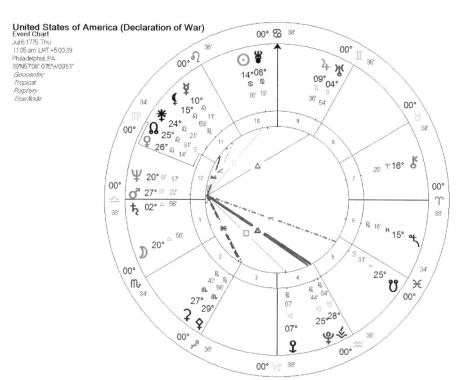

The US meets the world as the self-appointed equalizer, reconciler, and adjudicator. (Chart Ruler, Venus in Leo applying to a new phase semisextile Mars Virgo 12th)

Potential for the aggrandizement of self-worth. Need to proselytize and promote national beliefs and agendas. (Venus Leo 11th partile crescent sextile Jupiter Gemini 9th)

Periodic struggles finding self-worth and individuality within community. Probable future evolutionary paths include communities built upon principles of equality and humanitarianism. There is an ongoing process of self-actualized, often visionary individuation, magnetically drawn forward by traumatic memories from the past. (Venus Leo 11th House applying to a crescent square to Uranus Gemini 9th House)

Manifest Destiny, the Great American Dream, utopian vision, egalitarian governance. (Venus separating from a new phase conjunction to the Lunar North Node Leo 11th)

Isolationism, feeling different. (only a single aspect to an inner planet; applying to a new phase semisextile to Mars Virgo 12th)

Crises between myriad beliefs, the need to find communal balance. (Venus Leo applying to a 1st quarter square to Uranus Gemini 9th)

Conflicting tensions between individual expression and consensus necessity. (Venus Leo separating from a gibbous quincunx to Pluto Capricorn Rx 4th)

Projects as world role model. (Venus Leo separating from a 1st quarter trine to Chiron Aries 7th)

US Jupiter Gemini 9th House

Ruler of the 3rd House
MEDIA
POST OFFICE
TRANSPORTATION

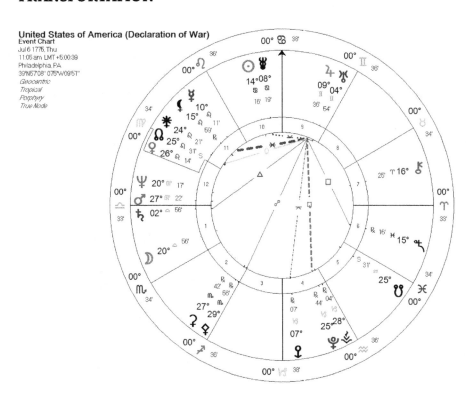

United States of America (Declaration of War)
Event Chart
Jul 6 1776, Thu
11:05 am LMT +5:00:39
Philadelphia, PA
39°N57'08" 075°W09'51"
Geocentric
Tropical
Porphyry
True Node

Strong focus on ideas and beliefs that can be forward-thinking; thinking that US national beliefs are best for the whole world, sense of national superiority. (Jupiter Gemini 9th separating from a new phase conjunction to Uranus Gemini 9th)
Opportunities for forward-looking, broad minded thinking and planning. (Mercury Leo 11th partile sextile Jupiter Gemini 9th)

Sense of justice, meeting the world with national self-authoritatively; furthering of national interests and beliefs to the exclusion of others. (Jupiter Gemini 9th separating from a last quarter trine to Saturn Libra 1st)

Exercise of power for national purpose that can disempower democracy. (Jupiter Gemini 9th applying to a full phase sesquisquare to Pluto Capricorn Rx 4th)
Events and circumstances that undermine and seek to redirect national beliefs. (Jupiter Gemini 9th applying to a full phase opposition to Eris Aries 7th)

Strong focus on ideas and beliefs that can be forward-thinking; thinking that US national beliefs are best for the whole world, sense of national superiority. (Jupiter Gemini 9th separating from a new phase conjunction to Uranus Gemini 9th)

Opportunities for forward-looking, broad minded thinking and planning. (Mercury Leo 11th partile sextile Jupiter Gemini 9th)

Sense of justice, meeting the world with national self-authoritatively; furthering of national interests and beliefs to the exclusion of others. (Jupiter Gemini 9th separating from a last quarter trine to Saturn Libra 1st)

Exercise of power for national purpose that can disempower democracy (Jupiter Gemini 9th applying to a full phase sesquisquare to Pluto Capricorn Rx 4th)

Events and circumstances that undermine and seek to redirect national beliefs. (Jupiter Gemini 9th applying to a full phase opposition to Eris Aries 7th)

Presidential manipulation of the judicial and electoral processes. (Sun Scorpio 2nd by transit separates from a gibbous quincunx to US Jupiter Gemini 9th)

Primary legal focus on the rule of law. (Venus Libra 1st by transit separates from a partile 1st quarter trine to US Jupiter Gemini 9th)

Struggles between democracy and authoritarianism, unilateral exercise of government power. (Saturn Capricorn 4th separates from a disseminating sesquisquare to US Jupiter Gemini 9th

Pluto Capricorn 4th from a disseminating sesquisquare to US Jupiter Gemini 9th)

Unresolved patterns of illegal activity within the Justice Department. (Eris Aries 7th separates from a partile balsamic semisquare to US Jupiter Gemini 9th)

US Saturn Libra 1st House

Ruler of the 4th House
REAL ESTATE, DEMOCRACY
Mundane Astrology:
ELDERLY
MINES

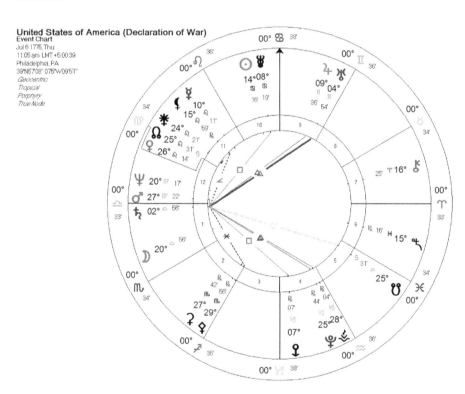

United States of America (Declaration of War)
Event Chart
Jul 6 1776, Thu
11:05 am LMT +5:00:39
Philadelphia, PA
39°N57'08" 075°W09'51"
Geocentric
Tropical
Porphyry
True Node

The sense of national authority is backed by a militarized world stance. The US meets the world as its police force.(Mars applies to a balsamic conjunction to Saturn Libra 1st , Saturn conjunct Ascendant 1st)

There are recurring legal crises between protecting the rights of property and protecting the rights of the individual. (Jupiter separates from last quarter trine to Saturn Libra 1st)

There is often an active political agenda to disseminate the virtues of the American culture in the world. (Saturn Libra 1st House applies to a 1st quarter trine to Uranus Gemini 9th)

Crises generated when power is exercised without restraint and deaf to the needs of the public at large. (Saturn Libra 1st House applies to a last quarter trine to Pluto Capricorn Rx 4th)

The exercise of authority needs to be balanced with the needs of the individual and the needs of the collective. (Saturn Libra 1st House separates from squares the lunar nodes)

Periodic upheavals to the country as a whole, the people at large, and the office of the Presidency. (Saturn Libra 1st House applies to a last quarter square to Eris in Capricorn Rx 4th)

US Neptune Virgo 12th House

Ruler of the 6th House
PUBLIC HEALTH
EPIDEMICS
WORK FORCE
Mundane Astrology:
SOCIALISM
DRUG PROBLEMS,
WELLBEING OF THE LESS ADVANTAGED

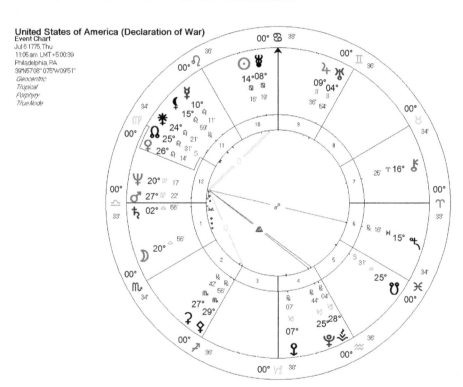

United States of America (Declaration of War)
Event Chart
Jul 6 1775, Thu
11:05 am LMT +5:00:39
Philadelphia, PA
39°N57'08" 075°W09'51"
Geocentric
Tropical
Porphyry
True Node

The struggle to provide the greatest good for the country and its people. (Moon Libra 1st by transit partile semisextile Neptune Virgo 12th)

Public actions and choices at their worst driven by selfish interest, clandestine illegal activities; At best driven by spiritual or metaphysical beliefs and practices. (Mars Virgo new phase conjunction Neptune Virgo 12th)

Evolutionary pressure driven by idealism and unconditional love; lawlessness and lack of public trust. (Pluto Capricorn Rx 4th applies to a 1st quarter trine to Neptune Virgo 12th, Neptune Virgo 12th semisextile Moon Libra 1st)

Can be a sacred commitment to the pursuit of ideals that strive to support the greater good. (Vesta Capricorn Rx 4th applies to a 1st quarter trine to Neptune Virgo 12th)

The Coming New Age Of Enlightenment?

The American political system, conceived as it was during the Age of Reason and Enlightenment, was the first working model of what was considered to be representative government in which power was shared equally between the government and the governed. Though our founding fathers had the right idea, the fragile political experiment they created seems to have been flawed from the onset. The political and social issues that we are facing today stem from the fact that the concept of "one man, one vote" was never achieved. In fact the vote was denied for almost two hundred years to women and people of color.

These issues are compounded by the fact that though the fore-runner to the US Constitution so forcefully stated that it was

> "self-evident, that all men are created equal, that they are endowed by their Creator with certain unalienable Rights, that among these are Life, Liberty and the pursuit of Happiness"

the legal endorsements of US Constitution ratified a decade later, focused on the rights of property, and failed to address the rights of the individual. It has taken almost 250 years of hard fought legal battles to accomplish what appears to have been the original intent of the colonial framers of independence. What we are now recognizing is the the Civil War is not over, and slavery never ended.

At the time of this writing, the American political system is currently experiencing pressures that the Founding Fathers did not foresee.

Printed in Great Britain
by Amazon

51643906R00092